# Author Biography

Mr. C.I.D Clark (JP) was born on 24 September 1946 at Kiagbodo town in Burutu Local Govt Council Area of Delta State, Nigeria. He attended Govt College, Ughelli, Delta State from 1960 to 1966 where he studied for his Ordinary and Advanced level certificates. He earned his WASC in 1964 and H.S.C.(A.L.) in 1966. Mr. Clark attended the University of Ibadan where he undertook his undergraduate studies in sociology from 1967 to 1970 and obtained a 2nd class Honours Upper division B.Sc. Degree in sociology. As a result of his impressive degree result, the authorities of the University of Ibadan sponsored Mr. Clark with a Rockefeller Foundation of New York scholarship to study a Masters in Sociology at Indiana University, Bloomington Indiana, USA; he graduated with an M.A. Degree in Sociology in 1974.

Mr. Clark is happily married to Dr. Mrs. Anthonia O. Clark, who is Head of the Department of the Vocational and Technical Education Faculty  of Education, University of Benin, Benin City, Nigeria, and they have six children and seven grand-children. Mr. Clark has been a lecturer and researcher at the University of Benin since January, 1976. Mr. Clark has also served in Government as an Honourable Commissioner for Education, and later for Health, in Delta State from February 1994 to November 1997.

# SOCIAL PSYCHOLOGY

**CYRIL I.D. CLARK**
University of Benin, Benin City, Nigeria.

Published 2011 by arima publishing

www.arimapublishing.com

ISBN 978 1 84549 496 4

© C I D Clark 2011

Printed and bound in the United Kingdom

Typeset in Palatino Linotype 12 pt.

Abramis is an imprint of arima publishing.

arima publishing
ASK House, Northgate Avenue
Bury St Edmunds, Suffolk IP32 6BB
t: (+44) 01284 700321

www.arimapublishing.com

# TABLE OF CONTENTS

# PREFACE

This book - **Social Psychology** - is a general introduction to the academic discipline called SOCIAL PSYCHOLOGY. The major objective of the book is to show the relatively distinctive nature, scope and significance of social psychology as an academic enterprise. It is hoped that this book will enable the reader - especially the beginning student of social psychology at the undergraduate, postgraduate, or diploma levels in the Universities, polytechnics, and other advanced educational institutions - to learn and acquire a fairly full, broad-based and intelligent knowledge and understanding of the overall nature, purpose, and relevance of social psychology as a social or human behavioural science subject.

**C.I.D. Clark (JP)**
Dept. of Sociology & Anthropology,
University of Benin,
Benin City.

# CHAPTER ONE

# THE FIELD OF SOCIAL PSYCHOLOGY

## SECTION (A)
## THE DISTINCTIVE NATURE OF SOCIAL PSYCHOLOGY

### (i)   INTRODUCTION

The academic discipline that we now know as social psychology had its beginnings in the later half of the nineteenth century in Europe and America, but as an academic discipline it probably did not begin to be formally taught and learnt until the 1890s and 1900s, also in Europe and America. Unlike its sister disciplines such as sociology and economics which are easily associated with one or two founding fathers, the emergence of social psychology may be attributed to the works of several founding fathers. The founding fathers of social psychology, that is, the various intellectuals whose seminal writings and/or teachings furnished the initial definitions, theories, and methodologies of social psychology include the Americans James Mark Baldwin, Charles Horton Cooley, George Herbert Mead, Edward A. Ross, and Floyd H, Allport; as well as the Europeans Gabriel Tarde (French), Gustave Le Son (French), Sigmund Freud (Austrian), and Williams McDougall (Briton).

The disciplined name probably first appeared in Baldwin's book, **Social and Ethical Interpretations in Mental Development: A Study in Social Psychology** (1897). In 1908, McDougall and Ross published the first full-fledged textbooks, which were exclusively devoted to presenting systematically the nature, scope, and objectives of social psychology. In 1924,

Allport published the next most influential full-scale textbook of social psychology. However, since the 1920s uptill now, numerous textbooks and definitive essays or monographs on the distinctive nature of social psychology have been published in several countries, Including the United States of America, Western Europe, India, and Australia.

As a result of these various developments, social psychology as we now know and study it in the contemporary, times, .has acquired a considerably broad and diversified meaning. An examination of a representative sample of standard definitions of social psychology by different internationally renowned social psychologists will show clearly and objectively, the relatively distinctive nature of social psychology, as a social or behavioural science subject.

## (ii)   DEFINITIONS OF SOCIAL PSYCHOLOGY

There are several different plausible definitions of social psychology. Some of the most notable common and up-to-date definitions of the discipline are, as follows:-

(1)   The American Social Psychologist Kimball Young defines social psychology in his textbook titled, **Handbook of Social Psychology** (Revised Edition, 1957: pages 1-3), as follows:-

> *"Social psychology is concerned with the study of the interactional processed of human beings. Some features of the (discipline) rest upon general psychology and others come from sociology and cultural anthropology. From the former (i.e. general psychology) we draw heavily for our understanding of the processes involved in motivation, learning, perception, and language. From the latter (that is, both sociology and anthropology) we make use of materials leaning on social organization and culture patterns. These latter provide much of the*

*content of what the individual learns as a member of his society or group. We might say that while our major emphasis is on the Individual in interaction with others, such interaction can only be understood within the societal and cultural matrix in which it occurs."*

(2)  The American Psychologist Gordon W. Allport defines social psychology in his article titled, "The Historical Background of Modern Social Psychology" published in Gardner Lindzey and Ellict Aronson (Editors), **The Handbook of Social Psychology** (Second-Edition, 1968: pages 1-80), as follows:-

With few exceptions, social psychologist, regard their discipline as an attempt to understand and explain how the thought, feeling, and behaviour of individuals are influenced by the actual, imagined, or implied presence of others. The term "implied presence" refers to the many activities the individual carries out because of his position (role) in a complex social structure and because of his membership in a cultural group." (Page 3; note that the underlinings are in the original text by Allport).

(3)  The three American Social Psychologists David Krech, Richard S. Crutchfeild, and Egerton L. Ballachey define Social Psychology in their textbook titled, Individual in Society: A textbook of Social Psychology (1962: page 5), as follows:-

Social psychology can be defined as the Science of interpersonal behaviour events. The goal of social psychology is to derive the laws of the development, change, and nature of interpersonal behaviour events." (Note that the underlinings are in the original textbook by David Kreech and Co.).

(4)     The Indian Social Psychologist B. Kuppuswamy defines social psychology in his textbook, titled Elements of Social Psychology (1973: Page 220) as follows:-

(Social Psychology) is the study of the members of a society in relation to that society. The study of the behaviour of individuals in groups.

(5)     The American Social Psychologist, Edwin P. Hollander defines social psychology in his textbook titled, Principles and Methods of. Social Psychology (Third Edition, 1976: pages 30-31), as follows:

Primarily, social psychology studies the psychology of the individual in society. This involves probing the many features of the social environment which, influence Individuals. Social psychology emphasises the part which the individual plays in social relationships, and it focuses on understanding the processes underlying these relationships. (Note that the underlinings are in the original text by Edwin P. Hollander).

## (iii)　A SUMMING UP OF THE DISTINCTIVE NATURE OF SOCIAL PSYCHOLOGY

On can actually see clearly from the above-mentioned five standard definitions of Social Psychology that all of them present identical conceptions of the distinctive nature of the discipline[1]. The most important elements which represent the distinctive nature of Social Psychology are, as follows:

(1)　Social psychology is a social scientific study;

(2)　Of the social and cultural factors - such as, social structures, social organizations, social interactions, social relationships, social beliefs, values, norms, and attitudes, incentives, and motivations that significantly influence.

(3)　All the different ways and manners in which individual human beings behave - such as the various individual feelings, perceptions, learnings, cognitions, impressions, values, norms, beliefs, attitudes, motivations, actions, achievements, happiness, failures, frustrations, angers, neuroses, schizophrenia, psychoses, and other behaviour patterns that different individuals display in their everyday lives in any society, such as Nigeria, Ghana, etc.; and

(4)　Vice versa.

---

[1]　It is not necessary for students to reproduce more than one or two of these (or rather) definitions of <u>social psychology</u> whenever they are asked to define social psychology in either a class assignment or in an examination.

# SECTION (B)
# A BRIEF HISTORY OF SOCIAL PSYCHOLOGY

For thousands of years men and women have recognized the fact that both individual human beings on the one hand, and human groups/ organizations/communities/societies on the other hand, represent relatively distinctive and separate units of social actions. That is, that either individuals or groups/societies, can initiate and/or react/respond to actions, and therefore exert varying degrees of positive and/or negative influences upon one another. For example, individuals like Moses of the Jews, Jesus of Nazareth, Mohammed of Arabia, Ambakederemo of the Ijos, etc, represent very great historic personalities, because they have been credited with having performed certain very heroic individual or personal acts which exerted a great deal of positive influences upon both their own contemporaries, as well as several generations of posterities. Similarly, the very profound and pervasive military, political, economic and diplomatic endeavours and successes of

(1)    the ancient Greek city-states, produced philosopher - kings, and professional military personalities;

(2)    the ancient Roman Empire produced imperious and bellicose leadership personalities (e.g., the Pompeiis, the Caesars, the Brutuses, etc); patricians; plebeians; and enslaved personalities;

(3)    the pre-colonial Benin Kingdom produced the imperious Benin monarchy; feudalistic Chiefs, fetish priests, commoners and eyienobas;

(4)    the egalitarian pre-colonial IJO clan-groups produced such individually very free, enterprising, and fabulously successful big merchants and business - organizers (e.g., the Ambakederemos, the Pepples, the Jajas, the Alagoas,

etc), as well as several other indolent, unenterprising, and poor individuals.

From time immemorial up to date, men and women have very painstakingly observed and quite critically reflected upon all of the several different specific ways and manners in which the various relatively independent behaviours of both groups/ societies and individuals exert varying degrees of reciprocal influences upon one another. Yet social psychology can be validly regarded as being a very new and modern human social/behavioural science discipline, which is not quite more than about one hundred or so years old. As a relatively full-fledged, unique, and Separate academic discipline, social psychology had what amounted to its preliminary beginnings or origins in the 1890s and 1900s in the United States of America and Western Europe. In other words, despite the fact that several different people across virtually the whole world have always recognized the relative differentness of individual actions on the one hand, and the differentness of group/organisational/ societal actions on the other hand; and then all of the several different ways in which both of these two sets of "social actors" influence one another since during the times of the ancient Ijos, Urhobos, Itsekiris, Binis, Igbos, Romans, Yorubas, Hausa-Fulanis, Arabs, Greeks, Jews, Aryans, Indians, Chinese, etc, it was only during the 1990s and 1900s that some perspicacious and enterprising American and European sociologists and psychologists succeeded in actually developing the relatively new and distinctive systematic social scientific discipline called "social psychology", which specifically seeks to study/analyze, and show exactly how and why the separate acts/behaviours of individuals, and those of groups/societies, influence one another.

I agree with the distinguished Nigerian historian Kenneth O. Dike who wrote in The Eminent Nigerians (1965), that we study history (i.e., the past) in order to understand the present in its proper perspective. I also agree with the American Social Psychologist Kimball Young's view (1957: pages 3-4) view that "as an academic discipline, social psychology is old enough to provide us with certain historical trends which may help us to understand the content(s) and boundaries of this discipline as they can be found in the contemporary times." The most important justification for regarding any one person as an important contributor to the development of social psychology is that any such person must have actually originated, discovered, or significantly expatiated and clarified any topic which has moved the discipline into some kind of new threshold of awareness and improvement in its basic professional aims, objectives, and endeavours. Therefore, it is necessary that every student of social psychology must always be able to constantly pin-point exactly how relevant whatever it is that is being credited to any contributor actually is to the major interests and preoccupations of social psychology - especially as stipulated by its definitions. These are some of the most crucial points which students must carefully note as they proceed to read the accounts on each one of all of the various individuals whom I have decided to regard as being among some of the most note-worthy contributors to the gradual development of the relatively new academic discipline called social psychology. For the sake of analytical convenience, I will classify this historical account of social psychology into two broad categories, as follows:-

(1)   The works and contributions of the founding fathers; and
(2)   The works and contributions of the modern/contemporary social psychologists.

## The Founding Fathers of Social Psychology

The expression "the founding fathers of social psychology" simply refers to all of the several different professional intellectuals as well as career-academicians who were the pioneer architects, whose seminal writings and/or teachings helped a great deal to provide the initial definitions, theories, and methodologies of social psychology, and who, therefore, contributed quite immensely to the establishment of this relatively new social science discipline. It is necessary for students to carefully note that since social psychology had not existed as a full-fledged academic discipline prior to the writings/ teachings of its founding fathers, it, therefore, obviously means that these so-called "founding fathers of social psychology" were not, themselves, originally trained in social psychology and some of them did not also even profess or practise social psychology (as we presently know it nowadays) during their own life times. Therefore, it is actually we ourselves contemporary, career-academic social psychologists who have read, assessed, and found out certain relevant ideas in the extent writings of these so-called "founding fathers", and which we have decided to regard as important and integral parts and parcels of our modern discipline. There are several different eminent social scientific scholars who can be validly regarded as "founding fathers" of modern social psychology. However, I will like to recognize and briefly discuss the salient contributions of only the following men towards the development of our modern-day social psychology.

## James Mark Baldwin:

Baldwin was an American psychologist and philosopher, who later turned to cultivate his professional academic interests in social psychology. He developed his interests and views on social psychology in two of his books, as follows:

(i)  <u>Social and Ethical Interpretations in Mental Development:
A Study in Social Psychology</u> (1897)
(ii)  <u>The Individual and Society</u> (1911).

Baldwin's major contributions to social psychology may be summarized, as follows:- Using a theory of imitation, suggestion, and accommodation (i.e., habits). Baldwin traced the relatively complex social processes which he believed were largely responsible for the gradual development of virtually every human Individual's set of behavioural traits, from birth through death. This social process is what we call "socialization" nowadays. But Baldwin had called it "the dialectic of personal growth", which, according to him, largely consists of the "give and take between the individual and his fellows". Most importantly, Baldwin deduced therefrom that there is a logical and rational unfolding of the "self" or "personality" under such a situation of social stimulation.

In sum, the major contribution which Baldwin made towards the development of modern social psychology is that his work largely foreshadowed many of the core issues which make up the topic of "socialization and the processes of personality development", which still undoubtedly represent some of the major and most important aspects or modern social psychology. Furthermore, Baldwin also exerted a great deal of direct influences upon two other very distinguished fellow American founding fathers of the discipline, namely, Charles Horton Cooley, and George Herbert Mead.

**Charles Horton Cooley (1864 - 1929)**
Cooley was an American economist, sociologist and social psychologist. He developed his ideas and contributions towards the development of social psychology in three of his books, as follows:-
(i)  Human Nature and The Social Order (1902)

(ii)   Social Organization: A Study of the Larger Mind (1909)

(iii)  Social Process (1918)

On the whole, Cooley shared the same basic and general outlook towards the patterns/networks of the relationships and interactions which exist between individuals and groups and societies as Baldwin. Like Baldwin, Cooley's major contentions were that (1) both individuals and groups or societies were very separate units of social actions, (2) but that both individuals, and groups/societies are also inextricably intertwined at the same time. In short, that individuals, groups and societies are complementary in the closest sense. Cooley also stamped his own relatively unique and impressive imprints on several other important aspects of the newly blossoming discipline - e.g., in the clarification of the epistemology of social psychology, socialization, personality development, and primary groups.

With regards to the epistemology of social psychology, during the time of Cooley - that is, around the end of the 19th century and the beginning of the present 20th century - it had been somehow fashionable in philosophical discourses to treat the question of exactly how both the "individual" and "society" relate to each other as being essentially a kind of "abstract" philosophical problem. As a result, many of the social philosophers of that time sought to ask and answer questions such as: To what extent does the Individual human being actually take on social values, norms, and other social behavioural traits? Why should any individual require any social behavioural traits at all? Etcetera.

Cooley was one of the few Western social scholars of that generation who was perspicacious and bold enough to express the view that the relation between the individual and society was not a subject for doubtful and abstract philosophical debates, but rather that it was a very concrete and empirical issue, and as such, that the most appropriate question which interested scholars should seek to ask and answer is: Exactly how and how does any one individual human being acquire the social behavioural ways of his/her society? Cooley himself also provided an answer to this question. For example, in his first book - <u>Human Nature and the Social Order</u> (1902) - Cooley traces out in considerable detail the way in which the human personality develops within the social matrix of family, play group, neighbourhood, and other primary groups. While in his second book - <u>Social Organization: A Study of the Larger Mind</u> (1909) - Coolly indicates the tremendous changes which occur in human personality as a result of the modern industrial age with its specialization of labour, its urbanization of population, its rapid communication, its class conflicts, and other conditions related to the breakdown of primary-groups influences upon the lives and welfares of individuals.

Thus, in the main, Cooley bequeathed to modern social psychology a number of very important ideas about how society moulds the 'behavioural' traits of individuals (which represent their various personalities) through the social processes of "socialization"; the key role which "primary-groups" - especially the "family" - play in such socialization; and also how certain macroscopic social processes (e.g., industrialization, urbanization, social stratification, etc) could also very significantly interfere with the normal micro-social contexts and of socialization and personality development. But probably the most memorable contribution which Charles Horton Cooley bequeathed to modern social psychology in his very famous and useful "looking-glass self" concept.

## GEORGE HERBERT MEAD (1863 – 1931)
Mead was an American philosopher and social psychologist. Throughout the greater part of his adult life, Mead was a full professor of philosophy at the University of Chicago (which has

always remained one of the best ten out of the several thousands of Universities which exist in the United States of America). There were also in the same Philosophy Department with him such then very famous philosophy professors - e.g., John Dewey, etc - whose then very new, radical, and popular ideas about "pragmatism", "language"', "education", etc influenced G.H. Mead a great deal. It was Mead, much more than anyone else, during their time, who actually clarified, illuminated, and brought out the distinctive nature of social psychology. Yet Mead himself published very little. His two or so extant books mainly consist of his students' compilations and publications of his lecture notes after he himself had died. The most remarkable one among them is called <u>Mind, Self, and Society</u> (1934).

Accepting the basic premises of both Baldwin and Cooley, and also strongly influenced by the then prevalent brands of functionalist and behaviouristic psychology, Mead was able to formulate a more or less "objective" social psychological perspective of the <u>social psychological</u> processes that are largely responsible for the emergence and operation of the human "self", or "personality". It was he who had first indicated the importance of "imitation" and "role-taking" in the development of human personality. Mead emphatically pointed out that both the "self" and the "social conscience" (i.e., "culture") were man-made social, phenomena, and not "nature-made" phenomena; and that both of them were simultaneously developed or produced during the continuous social interaction processes which make up "socialization" and "education". In this regard, Mead also drew special attention to the crucial part which "language" also plays in the developments of both an individual's personality as well as a group/society's culture. For, according to Mead, it is language - which largely consists of "symbols" - which serves as the very vital and indispensable medium, which enables human beings to learn/acquire the "roles" and the "perspectives" or "values" of one another. That through "role taking", "role playing", and the like, both the "self" and the "generalized others" gradually develop. And that the "generalized others" in general, and the "significant others" in particular, constitute the basic social structure of the social behavioural traits which each individual learns and internalizes, and which also thereby represent the basic structure of any individual's behavioural traits, which make up his/her basic personality structure, which subsequently determines, influences or governs the various ways and manners in which any individual behaves in his/her society.

Although, in the main, Mead, like Baldwin, Cooley, and the like, also very much emphasized that both the "individual" and "society" are complementary to each other in the closest sense, but unlike both Baldwin and Cooley, Mead also made some frantic but largely inchoate and futile attempts to also recognize that there is- also a nonsocial (i.e., a biological), spontaneous, unpredictable, and influential aspect of each individual human being's personality structure. Mead continuously stressed that biological/subjective/inner/ individualistic aspect of each individual's personality is the major source of his/her overt social behaviours. He argued that men/women are not just like ordinary robots/puppets, who mostly act in accordance with only how other people direct them, but rather that each individual possesses his/her own unique behavioural patterns, which largely govern/guide how each individual behaves most of the time in the society. This unique/individualistic aspect of any person's personality, Mead called the "I", while he called the other aspect of the individual's personality structure which consists of all of the social-cultural behavioural traits which the individual has learnt and acquired from his/her significant and generalized others, the "me".

However, we can learn from a detailed analysis of "socialization and the processes of personality development", that it was the very versatile Jewish-Austrian Sigmund Freud who had actually first succeeded in systematically developing and providing us with a truly explicit and accurate theory which very clearly and intelligently isolates both the purely "individualistic" and also the purely "social-cultural" aspects which always co-exist in varying proportions within the basic personality structure of every individual human being.

## Sigmund Freud (1856 - 1939)

Freud himself was, very much like his personality theory, a very realistic, extremely egoistical or individualistic gentleman. He was a Jew, born in Freiberg, Moravia, but he spent the lengthiest period of his quite long life, up until 1938, in Vienna, the Capital City of Austria, Europe. Freud was forced to flee Vienna in 1938, when the belligerent and predative Nazi-German military men and women conquered and occupied Austria during the Second World War. As a result of that Freud spent the last one year of his life in England. If we are to mention the first five or six men whose very prodigious intellectual endeavours have exerted the most profound, pervasive, and enduring influences upon all of humanity as a whole, Sigmund Freud, will be one of them. The others are William Shakespeare, Isaac Newton, Karl Marx, Thomas Edison, John Maynard Keynes, and Albert Einstein. Three out of these six - that is, Karl Marx, Albert Einstein, and Sigmund Freud - are men of Jewish descent.

As one of the founding fathers of psychology, Freud is particularly noted for being the founder of one of its most distinguished and extremely popular branches called psychoanalysis.

Sigmund Freud was originally trained in medicine and received his medical degree from the University of Vienna in

1881, He had intended to pursue a career as a research scientist, but instead, being a realistic and pragmatic man, he felt obliged to enter into medical practice, in order for him to be able to earn enough money to maintain himself and his family. He practiced under the French Physician named Jean Charcot, who dabbled extensively into hypnosis; and then also under Josef Breuer, who was a specialist in mentally disturbed patient's". During those periods, Freud became fascinated with psychology, and as a result he decided to devote the rest of his professional career towards an effort to develop and produce a more realistic and useful theory of personality which will, hopefully, help to better explain the very complex and dynamic nature of the human personality, than all of the then hitherto fashionable personality theories - e.g., the theories by G.H. Mead, etc.

Freud was a versatile and prolific writer. He never hesitated to pronounce outside his subject, upon a wide gamut of topics – e.g., religion, sex, dreams, fantasies, women, human groups, illusions, history, literature, biography, etc. Thus Freud could be said to have been an intellectual in the truly classical tradition. However, his numerous and varied contributions to social psychology may be summarize under <u>four</u> major areas; all of them are integral component parts of the psycholoanalytic theoretical and methodological school of psychology that he founded.

(i)    Freud's theory of the tripartite structure of the human personality;

(ii)   Freud's theory of the role of the "unconscious" mechanism in the dynamic functioning of the human personality;

(iii)  Freud's theory of human psychosexual development; and

(iv)   Freud's psychoanalytic method of psychotherapy. Freud also coined and bequeathed an impressive wealth of concepts to social psychology, which include the following:- "Id", "Superego", "Ego", the "unconscious", "subconscious", "conscious", "displacement", "condensation", "dreams", "oedipus complex", "electra complex", "pleasure principle", "reality principle", "libide", "illusions", "delusions", "repressed drives", "aggression", etc, etc.

## Gustave Le Bon

Le Bon was a Frenchman, a psychologist, and social psychologist. He is chiefly associated with social psychology because of his epochal and seminal theory of crowd behaviour, which he propounded in his classical book titled The Crowd: A Study of the Popular Mind (1895). In his very brilliant and masterly essay titled "The Historical Background of Modern Social Psychology" (1954, 1968), the American social psychologist Gordon W. Allport, notes that "perhaps the most influential book ever written in social psychology is Le Bon's "The Crowd." That might be a slightly exaggerated opinion, but it is not too far from the real truths. The real truth is that Le Bon's The Crowd is indisputably one of the four or so most perceptive, controversial, influential and enduring classics in the discipline up until today. The others include S. Freud's The Interpretation of Dreams (19    ), G.H. Mead's Mind, Self, and Society (1934), and B.F. Skine   Walden Two (1948).

The terms "crowds" or "collective behaviour" generally refer to all of the several different forms, of relatively spontaneous, unstructured, unorganized, volatile; and ephemeral sequences of human social behaviour which transpire between any set of individuals by virtue of the fact that they are simultaneously involved in any relatively problematic, unstructured and unorganized social interaction situation - such as "crowds", "publics'", "demonstrations", "riots", "rebellions", "revolts", and "revolutions". In other words, "crowds" or "collective behaviour" are "quasi-groups". They represent very important substantive aspects of social life, as well as units of analysis in social psychology. It was the French Psychologist Le Bon who pioneered the social psychological study of "crowds" in particular and "collective behaviour" in general. That effort has earned him the invaluable credit and honour of his being generally recognized as the founding father of the modern "social psychology of collective behaviour."

Le Bon used the term "crowd" in a very broad or general sense, as a kind of synonym for the same modern-day social psychological terms of "collective behaviour", "collective dynamics", or "quasi-groups". However Le Bon's typology of crowds is not quite identical with our modern-day typologies. For example, he classified crowds into two major categories - namely, (i) Heterogeneous crowds, and (ii) homogenous crowds. For each category, he also distinguished certain specific types of crowds, as follows:-

## Table 1/1: Le Bon's Classification of Crowds

| Major Categories of Crowds | Specific Types of Crowds |
|---|---|
| 1. Heterogeneous Crowds | (1) Anonymous crowds (street crowds, for example). <br> (2) Crowds not anonymous (juries, parliamentary assemblies, etc). |
| 2. Heterogeneous Crowds | (1) Sects (political sects), religious sects, etc. <br> (2) Castes (the military caste, the priestly caste, the working caste, etc). <br> (3) Classes (the middle classes, the peasant classes, etc). |

It will be instructive for the interested contemporary student of "the social psychology of collective behaviours" to compare and contrast Le Bon's 19th century classification of crowds with any of the notable modern-day classifications of crowds, such as the ones by the French historian-sociologist George Rude (1964), the American sociologists Kurt Lang and Gladys E. Lang (1961), the American sociologist Neil Smelser (1964), the American sociologist James B. McKee (1974), and the Nigeria Social Psychologist Cyril I.D. Clark (1985).

Le Bon's classification of crowds way be relatively dated, but his theory of "crowed behaviour" is definitely not. Infact, his explanation of how and why crowds behave in their peculiarly spontaneous, unstructured and volatile manner, is the really seminal and immortal aspect of his whole work on crowds. Le Bon largely based his theory of crowd behaviour on the concept of "suggestion" (that is, "the hysteric splitting of personality"), and he described it as follows:-

> "... the individual may be brought into such condition that, having entirely lost his conscious personality, he obeys all the suggestions of the operator (that is, the crowd) who has deprived him of it, and commits acts in utter contradiction with his character and habits." (page 34).

According to Le Bon, crowd conditions release deep prejudices, racial tradition and brute instinct. And that the typical individual who is participating in a crowd

> "... is no longer conscious of his acts. In his case, as in the case of the hypnotized subjects, at the same time that certain faculties are destroyed, others may be brought to a high degree of exaltation. Under the influence of a suggestion, he will undertake the

accomplishment of certain acts with irresistible impetuosity." (p. 35).

Le Bon says that both the leaders and the mass-members/participants of any crowd are usually mostly given to constant <u>action,</u> but never to critical <u>thought.</u> That whenever a person joins a crowd, he descends several rungs in the ladder of civilization. His explanation for that kind of drastic change in an individual's behaviour is that, when any person is isolated or alone, he tends to reason of think before acting, but that whenever he is in a crowd, he will tend to act by instinct, by virtue of the fact that his attention or consciousness will be tied to the ones of the other fellow members of the crowd, especially to that of the crowd's leader(s). It is also quite instructive to note that Le Bon also believed so much in the excessive suggestibility of women, and of certain races or ethnic groups that, using them as a metaphor, he said that "crowds are everywhere distinguished by feminine characteristics, and that Latin crowds are the most feminine of all."

Lastly, but not the least, Le Bon also addressed himself to the issue of the social functions of crowds. He expressed very low opinions about the social functions of crowds. He said that crowds are largely a menace to established social institutions, and that crowds flourish as civilization declines. Le Bon compared the "crowd" to a herd of cattle. He called them a pack of "riffraffs", and blamed them for always seeking to destroy and hark any free-enterprise and progressing society back to "primitive communism". On the whole, in all of his considerations of the functions of crowds, in society or history, Le Bon expressed very strong anti-socialist or anti-democratic sentiments. But despite all of his criticisms against crowds, he did not, in the final analysis, condemn them completely. For example, while Le Bon was deploring the irrationality of "electoral crowds", and the like, he still said that it might be well to risk their errors, largely on the ground that crowds do, in their own way, express the basic aspirations of their own people or society, and, that at times, they may even do so with some appreciable measure of heroism or success.

Le Bon's relatively conservative and controversial theory of-crowd behaviour has left an indelible imprint on virtually all of the other major subsequent theories or analyses of crowd behaviours up to date. In fact, virtually every relatively major contemporary theory or analysis of crowds in particular, or collective behaviours in general, has been largely developed within or in tension with Le Bon's classical theory.

# SECTION (C)
## SOCIAL PSYCHOLOGY AND ALLIED DISCIPLINES

From the discipline's compound name which is made up of the two words of "SOCIAL" and "PSYCHOLOGY", any relatively curious student might wish to know whether there is any special connection or relationship which exists between "social psychology" and other social or behavioural sciences - e.g.; sociology, social-cultural anthropology, psychology, or the like - whose names also have one synonym or the other with either one of the two component parts of the name SOCIAL PSYCHOLOGY. The standard correct answer is yes. The several different major connections which exist between social psychology and these other three subjects are as follows:-

(a)    **Social Psychology and General Psychology:**
    General Psychology, or simply, Psychology, is the scientific study of the behaviour and relaxed mental processes of individual human beings. The primary aim of general psychology is to study the behaviour of individuals in order to find out the salient factors which determine or influence them. It uses scientific methods to collect data in order to study behaviour. By using such methods a large body of knowledge concerning the processes of perception, learning, attitudes, intelligence, motivation, cognition, personality, abnormal behaviour, etc has now been obtained. But the individual lives and grows up in groups. In fact, many cannot live without other people. Men live in families, in groups, in communities, and in nations. It is the other people in the family who not only bring up the child but also give him the language he uses, help to set the standards of his conduct; and teach him some of the important instrumental role a which he has to play in life, by rewarding him when he does well and by punishing him when

30

he does not. <u>The study of the individual in his interactions with others in any human society is the task of social psychology</u>. It is interested in the study of the formation of groups, type and functions of groups, and group dynamics. It is interested in the study of the several different ways and manners in which various human group behaviours, and the characteristics of human groups themselves change from time to time. The field of social psychology is primarily devoted to the understanding and the explanation of the individual's basic psychological processes - such as feeling, striving, perceiving, and learning - as they occur within the social and cultural contexts of any one human society - e.g, Nigeria.

Thus, the main difference between general psychology and social psychology is that the former claims to be able to study and explain the behaviours of individuals by themselves, while social psychology seeks to study individual behaviours in terms of the socio-cultural factors which significantly influence them. Just as the biologist studies the individual animal, and just as the physiologist studies the body of the individual human being, the general psychologist also can study the behaviour of the individual irrespective of the group in which he has been brought up. <u>But social psychology greatly extends our knowledge of the individual by studying his behaviour in the group situation, how he interacts with others, and how he is influenced by other people</u>. From this point of view, social psychology is related more to other social sciences, like sociology and social/cultural anthropology than to the biological science, while general psychology is related more to the biological sciences, than to the social sciences. <u>For example, while general psychology is interested in the development of personality as such, social psychology</u> is interested in the study of how personality is influenced <u>by social environments and social processes.</u> Social psychology is interested in the study of how the innate needs of man are modified by social and cultural influences, how social learning takes place and how an individual becomes a typical member of a group so that he not only speaks the particular language of the group in which he has been brought up but also acquires much of the attitudes which prevail in the group, and also cherishes the beliefs and values of that group; how he acquires the prejudices of the group and develops hostility towards other groups.

(b)     **Social Psychology and Sociology.**

The major aim of sociology is to study society and social organizations, how human beings create and recreate the organizations which guide and control much of their collective behaviours. Its main concern is to show how any society is organized, how it may succeed or fail to cope up effectively with the various social problems which always afflict it - e.g., lack of adequate food, crime, etc. Sociology studies how any society as an organization may deliberately or inadvertently encourage or stultify various motives and activities of virtually all of its diverse members, how it sets up certain laws or standards of behaviours, and why some of its citizens will obey them, while the others do not.

Sociology studies society as a system of usages and procedures, of authority and obedience, and how it succeeds or fails to control certain types of so-called dangerous and harmful human behaviours. Sociology studies social relationships, and how social relationships change, and how numerous and diverse types of individuals depend on the society for their protection, comfort, education, jobs, etc. Human beings live in groups, in communities, or in nations. Thus, the main difference between sociology and social psychology may be summarized as follows. Sociology is largely interested in all of the several different social structures and social relationships which can be found in any one human society **in themselves**, while social psychology is mostly interested in the several **different individuals who are involved in all of such social structures and social relationships**. Consequently, the crucial difference between these two disciplines lies with the focus or perspective of each of them. Both of them are also very much complementary in several very important ways. For example, every social relationship or interaction involves **attitudes** on the part of the individuals who enter into such relationships. Two persons may be friendly or hostile in their attitude to each other. That means that the social interaction or relationship between the two persons is obviously influenced by the attitude which each has towards the other. Similarly, any one human group as a whole may also develop attitudes towards any other group. For example, when there is a border dispute between any two or more ethnic groups in the country; each of the groups would tend to become hostile to the other group, and as a result, social tensions and social conflicts would invariably arise. Whether groups are family groups, village groups, linguistic groups, communal groups, or pressure groups, they develop attitudes of friendliness or indifference or hostility towards one another. Inter-tribal conflicts, inter-village conflicts, or international conflicts arise out or such hostile attitudes. Similarly, friendly attitudes within/or between groups also help to promote group cooperation. The task of social psychology is to study such "attitudes", how they arise, how they change or how they may resist any kind of change. While, on the other hand, sociology would be more interested in the social structures, social relationships, and social institutions themselves. It is obvious that the analytical interests of both of these two social sciences overlap a great deal in practically every aspect of social life or human behaviour which they study.

## (c) **Social Psychology and Social (or Cultural) Anthropology**

Anthropologists are usually mostly interested in the social institutions. The beliefs, values, norms - in short, the traditions and customs - or tribal societies, such as traditional Ijo, Urhobo, Bini, or Igbo societies. According to anthropologists, all of the things, which the members of any such societies have produced, whether it is an artifact or a taboo, an implement for work, or a mode of worship, in short, whether they are physical objects, or social and religious ideas or relationships, they all form "a culture". Thus, for the anthropologist, culture signifies the total social heritage of mankind. In their study of tribal groups, the anthropologists have become acutely aware of the intimate relation between the individuals and the culture itself. They have cone to realize that the understanding of the personality of the individual belonging to a culture as well as the cultural context or matrix of which the individual is a part demands a careful analysis of the ways in which the two are interrelated. In other words, social/cultural anthropologists have very extensively and convincingly shown that personality and culture are not only interrelated but are interdependent. Thus, we see the resemblances and differences between social psychology and social/cultural anthropology. Studies in social/cultural anthropology have shown how the perceptions and learnings of an individual are closely determined by their various specific cultural backgrounds. Thus, much of the factual data which have been collected by social/cultural anthropologists are of immense help in understanding how the personalities and behaviours of individuals are significantly influenced by social and cultural factors.

# SECTION (D)
# THE MAJOR ANALYTICAL OBJECTIVES OF SOCIAL PSYCHOLOGY

Social psychology, like every other academic/ professional discipline, has its own relatively distinctive set of analytical objectives, which usually guide its various students/experts in their various studies/ analyses of its various substantive subject-matters. Social psychology's analytical objectives consist of a number of intellectual commitments - theoretical and methodological - which are usually shared by the generality of professional social psychologists. The analytical objectives of social psychology show exactly the specific types of concrete empirical subject-matters which social psychologists select to study/analyze from time to time; the specific type of research methods and theoretical perspectives which they utilize, and the specific types of concrete and useful findings or results which they actually produce from time to time. Finally, the relatively distinctive set of the analytical objectives or commitments of social psychology represent the most basic and important evidences, clues or yardsticks, which any person can use to identify, apprise, and/or evaluate the distinctive nature and contributions of the discipline to humanity's knowledge about human behaviours, and attitudes vis-a-vis the nature and contributions of other extant disciplines.

On the whole, there are **five** major analytical objectives of social psychology, as follows:-

## (1)   Social Psychology Mostly Focuses Upon Psychosocial Phenomena

The special field of study of Social Psychology is the interplay or the intersection between any individual human being and any human group, organization, community, or society. All of the several different kinds of things which individuals do jointly with, or share together with, groups, organizations, communities, or societies represent **psychosocial phenomena** - for example, roles, statuses, attitudes, values, beliefs, norms, laws, prejudices, stereotypes, love, hatred, motivation, crime, delinquency, neuroses, psychoses, schizophrenia, knowledge, language, culture, marriage, divorce, etc. It is these and the several other similar kinds of psychosocial phenomena which explicitly and significantly involve the simultaneous acts or behaviours of both individuals and social systems that constitute the mainstay of the distinctive subject-matters of Social Psychology.

How does one know exactly whether a social psychologist is actually dealing with the psychosocial aspects of human behaviours or not? In other words, how should a student of social psychology know how to identify and focus upon the interplay or intersection between the acts of individual human beings on the one hand, and the acts of groups/organizations/ communities/societies on the other hand? Well, as I had shown earlier under section (C); unlike sociology, social/ cultural anthropology, and psychology, social psychology does the following which show that it is focusing exclusively upon the psychosocial aspects of human behaviours:-

(1)  In its analysis of any human behaviour, social psychology focuses on the attributes of individuals, while it ignores or at least de-emphasizes the "structural features" of the social-cultural context, in which any individual's behaviour occurs. This represents one of the major fundamental ways in which social psychology differs remarkably from both sociology and anthropology. It can be illustrated by examining any of the several different concrete examples which can be drawn from several different kinds of social institutional studies. For example, in the studies of social stratification, sociologists and

anthropologists tend to mostly focus upon the "objective" and "social-structural" manifestations of social stratification, while social psychologists would mostly tend to focus upon a people's "subjective" perceptions of their social classes and statuses vis-a-vis those of other people.

(2) In the analysis of the behaviour of individuals, social psychologists mostly attempt to describe and/or explain their conducts and motivations in terms of the relevant social-cultural factors which significantly influence them. In particular, the social psychologist looks for and seeks to clearly show in his analysis exactly <u>how</u> and <u>why</u> the external conduct and the inner life of individuals interplay with those of the other individuals with whom they engage in any form of purposeful social interaction. Furthermore, social psychologists also attempt to study closely and to analyze the several different personality types which can be found in any human society, and to explain them largely in terms of their inter-relations with the social structure and culture of their society.

One can actually see clearly from the above-mentioned examples, that the special field of study or focus in social psychology is always **the attitudes, and behaviours and of individuals as they are influenced by their societies**. As a result, the fundamental conception, or the directing idea, in social psychology is that of "social role". The key concept of "role" represents the most fundamental and important bridge which connects any individual behaviour with any group or societal event at any particular point in time.

Consequently, in striving to analyze any individual behaviour, a social psychologist focuses upon roles - that is, whatever any individual actually does, under any given social-cultural context. By focusing mainly on "roles," any social psychologist is able to simultaneously touch upon both the relevant "'social context" (in which the role was enacted), as well as the relevant "psychological aspect" (that is, the individual's "act" or "behaviour", itself).

## (2)    Social Psychology Seeks to Provide Relatively Scientific, Systematic, and Reliable Sets of Knowledge About Human Behaviour

There are several different sources of information about human behaviour across the whole world. However, there are four major types of such sources, as follows:- (a) common sense knowledge; (b) myths and proverbs; (c) literature, and all of the other arts subjects; and (d) science. As I had earlier pointed out above in Section (B), social psychology is a social science - that is, it mainly utilizes scientific methods and techniques of research and analysis to gather and analyze its various sets of information about human behaviour. From their scientific researches and analyses, social psychologists produce various sets of scientific information or ideas about human behaviour which are by far much more factual, accurate, objective, systematic, defensible, and useful (for any purpose whatsoever) than the types of information or ideas which may be obtained from any of the other above-mentioned sources of information.

## (3)    Social Psychology Mostly Studies and Analyzes Human Behaviour Holistically.

The concept of "holism" simply refers to the heuristic device or approach towards the study/analysis of any phenomenon – e.g., prejudices or attitudes of individuals towards anything, corruption in a society, forms of religious worshipping, victory in an election, etc - in which the analyst regards that phenomenon as an integral part of certain other related types of phenomena, which significantly influence or determine the specific way or manner in which that particular phenomenon which is being studied/analyzed has occurred in reality. Therefore, to study or analyze anything – e.g., human behaviour "holistically" mean's that the analyst actually examines and explains that thing in terms of the relevant variables of the larger external social and cultural context in which that thing has occurred; and the analyst also actually emphasizes the relations between the various component parts or elements to one another and to the totality of the social context.

Social psychologists mainly study or analyze human behaviour holistically, in the sense that they do not study/analyze any human behaviour as if it occurs in a vacuum or in isolation, but rather they study/analyze every form of human behaviour - e.g., the attitudes of individuals about inflation, nepotism, a good or bad government, free education or free health-care delivery services, armed robbery, poverty, sexual matters, etc - within and in terms of the specific historical period, and the specific societal and cultural contexts in which it has actually occurred. The major reason why it is extremely necessary and important for social psychologists to study/analyze human behaviour holistically is that all of the several different forms of human behaviours or social phenomena which ever occur, are actually made to occur in whatever forms that they occur by the particular historical period, and the particular societal and cultural contexts in which they occur. Therefore, by studying/ analyzing human behaviour holistically social psychologists endeavour to find out and show exactly how any one particular historical period, and societal and cultural contexts have actually significantly influenced and imparted their own relatively distinctive characteristics and identify onto the observed features of any one particular form of human behaviour or psychosocial phenomenon - such as the different attitudes of most members of society towards different types of political/military leaders, attitudes towards work, the practice of tribalism or nepotism, crime or delinquency, etc.

## (4)    Social Psychology Seeks to Analyze Human Behaviour Skeptically

The key term here is "skepticism". Skepticism means a doubting or questioning attitude or state of mind. It is the philosophical doctrine which states that knowledge about anything whatsoever – e.g., about human behaviour, how to split an atom, etc - is impossible, and that as a result any serious, realistic, and meaningful empirical inquiry about the nature of any empirical phenomenon – e.g., how and why human beings behave in whichever way or manner that they behave, at any particular point in time and place - must be conducted through the procedure in which one withholds accent until one has obtained a significant amount of supporting concrete evidence or proof about the actual nature of the occurrence of any one particular psychosocial phenomenon. Skepticism is one of the integral philosophies or principles of the scientific methodology which social psychologists and all other social or behavioural science researchers apply in their studies of human behaviours, and also in their provision of bodies of scientific knowledge about human behaviours.

Therefore, social psychologists usually mainly study or analyze human behaviours in a relatively skeptical, critical, objective, and unemotional way and manner. As a result, social psychologists do not easily believe or accept any fragmentary or superficial "common sense" or "official" accounts or explanations about any one of the numerous social, political, economic, religious, educational, or other things which occur around all of us in our groups, organizations, communities, or societies. But rather, this scientific skeptical attitude enables the social psychologist to doubt and withhold his belief in anything that he hears or reads about, until he has actually found out some adequate amount of supporting empirical evidence or proof about the nature of that thing. This attitude of scientific skepticism enables the social psychologist to see in a new and much more accurate or realistic light what he might have just taken for granted or on its possibly very fake face value. The utilization of the skeptical approach in social psychology for studying, analyzing, and interpreting human behaviour is sometimes called the "debunking" function of social psychology.

(5)    **Social Psychology is a Basic Social Science; and as a Result, it Mostly Seeks to Analyze Any Human Behaviour or Social Phenomenon as an End in Itself**

The statement that "Social Psychology is a basic social science" is a very weighty and important statement indeed. This statement, means that social psychology mostly seeks to study/analyze and produce-ordinary basic or objective information about any of the several different ways and manners in which individuals actually behave in their various groups, organizations, communities, or the larger society as a whole, at any particular point in time. These types of "objective scientific" information about human behaviour may also be called "positive statements". They largely show exactly **how individual have actually behaved, and not how they should or ought to behave**. The statements which predominantly show how individuals or people should or ought to behave in their groups, organizations, communities, or the larger society as a whole, are called "normative statements". Social psychologists mostly aim at producing "positive" or "scientific" statements, while avoiding making "normative" or "value-ladden" statements.

It is politicians, directors, administrators, managers, law enforcement agents (e.g., policemen), social welfare workers, teachers, husbands, wives, parents, lovers, elders, friends, clergymen, psychiatrists, brothers, sisters, children, diviners, oracle men, moral and religious proselytisers, etc, who have the freedom - depending only on the specific customs and traditions of each community/ society - to make "normative statements", which seek to direct, guide, or constrain the behaviours of the various individuals who are either friendly with related to, or under their authorities. However, the factual empirical statements about human behaviours - for example, about why certain individuals commit crimes, suicides, etc - which emerge from the painstaking empirical researches of social psychologists can and should be applied by all of the above-mentioned categories of practical people whenever they wish to direct or guide the behaviours of the various individuals with whom they are interacting. That is because, when such neutral factual scientific ideas about human behaviours are applied in guiding concrete human behaviours, individuals may really tend to behave in much more refined, positive, and socially beneficial ways and manners.

## SOCIAL PSYCHOLOGY AS A HUMANISTIC AND SCIENTIFIC ENDEAVOUR

The expression "social psychology as a humanistic and scientific endeavour" means that social psychology **consists** of elements of both the humanities and the sciences. Social psychology is humanistic in the sense that its substantive subject matters consist of "human behaviour", or "human affairs", and it is scientific in the sense that it utilizes scientific methods and techniques to conduct empirical research and obtain "objective facts" about human behaviour; and also to analyze them objectively and impartially. As a result, social psychology (like any of the other social/behavioural sciences) always simultaneously involves both a humanistic and scientific endeavour. Both the humanistic (that is, the substantive subject matters) and the scientific (that is, the methodological and theoretical) aspects of social psychology are complementary, and mutually inter-related. A combination of both of them makes up the total nature of social psychology.

The nature and scope of the humanistic aspects (that is, the substantive subject-matters) of social psychology can be delineated by identifying some of the topics which most social psychologists study and analyze. These include, social-cultural influences on individuals perceptions of people and objects; individuals conformity to group values and norms; attitudes formation and changes; public opinion formation and changes; the role of mass communication, propaganda, and coercive persuasion (that is, brainwashing) in the behaviour of individuals; aggression; group structure, dynamics, and leadership; intergroup tensions, prejudices, and discriminations; comparative social psychological studies of human behaviour in different cultures; and others.

Similarly, the nature and scope of the scientific aspects (that is, the research methods and theoretical perspectives) of social psychology can also be likewise delineated by identifying the major scientific research methods and theoretical perspectives which most social psychologists use for gathering and analyzing their empirical data about the behaviour of individuals in their various social-cultural settings. Largely because the scientific nature of social psychology is complex and involves several technical details, it is discussed separately in the following section, in order for the reader to obtain a reliable understanding of it.

# THE SCIENTIFIC NATURE OF SOCIAL PSYCHOLOGY

As I had earlier indicated above in section (B), social psychology is a social or human behavioural science subject. Any science subject - be it physics, chemistry, biology, medicine, engineering, sociology, economics, political science, psychology, or social psychology - is a relatively organised and systematic body of knowledge, which has been very carefully and painstakingly accumulated together, and which posits a series of relatively logically inter-connected statements, largely in the forms of hypotheses or propositions and models or theories, about the nature of the recurrent behaviours and inter-relationships between some concrete elements of some aspect of the universe.

Systematic body of knowledge, which has been very carefully and painstakingly accumulated together, and which posits a series of relatively logically inter-connected statements, largely in the forms of hypotheses or propositions and models or theories, about the nature of the recurrent individual behaviours of as well as of the inter-relationships between the various behaviours of individuals in their various groups, organizations, communities, or the larger society as a whole.

Every science subject - e.g., social psychology - is airways made up of two major complementary parts, as follows:-

(1)  Research Methodology and
(2)  Theoretical Analysis.

## (1)    The "Research Methods" of Social Psychology

The "research methods" of social psychology refer to the various specific practical scientific ways in which social psychologists actually observe, gather together, measure, quantify, process, and systematically arrange together, all of the several different bits and pieces of <u>concrete empirical scientific facts</u> which apparently represent the several different ways and manners in which various individuals actually behave or relate to one another in their various groups, organizations, communities, or societies. There are about <u>eight</u> major separate specific methods or approaches which any social psychologist may adopt to conduct an empirical research, for the purpose of obtaining some concrete empirical facts about any aspect of human behaviours, as follows:-

(a)     the Archival and/or Library research method;
(b)     the Survey research method;
(c)     the Field research method;
(d)     the Natural experimental research method;
(e)     the Quasi-experimental research method;
(f)     the Field experimental research method;
(g)     the Simulation research method; and
(h)     the Laboratory experimental research method.

Largely because of both space and time limitations, I will not be able to discuss the specific details of each of the above-mentioned eight research methods of social psychology in this present essay[2].   However, it should suffice it for me to only mention here that all of these different specific social psychological research methods involve the systematic study of any chosen aspect of the substantive subject matters of the discipline in such a way as to maximize a truthful rendition of the facts which can be associated with that particular aspect at any particular point in time. Preconceived ideas and/or biases are excluded, from the scientific search for the facts about any of

------

[2]     I have presented and discussed the specific details about each of these eight research methods in a separate essay titled "The Research Methods of Social-Psychology" (1983). That essay may be made available by special request to me. Chapter two in the textbook titled <u>Social Psychology,</u> by Lawrence S. Wrightsman is also a very good source for any interested student to learn more about the research methods of social psychology.

the substantive subject matters of social psychology as much as possible. It is largely by using any one of the above-mentioned eight research methods (or any other one) that social psychologists obtain and present the various concrete empirical facts about how and why various Individuals actually behave or relate to one another in their various groups, organizations, communities, or societies, from time to time.

## (2)    The Theoretical Perspectives of Social Psychology

The "theories/analyses" of social psychology refer to the various specific practical scientific ways in which social psychologists actually analyze and interpret the various empirical facts which they obtain from their various empirical researches, and thereupon show as logically and systematically as possible exactly how and why various individuals behave and relate to one another in their various concrete social-cultural contexts. Social psychologists do not just analyze and explain the social-cultural behaviours of individuals in anyhow way or manner, but rather they do so from some relatively well defined and defensible standpoints - which are what are commonly called the theoretical approaches or perspectives of social psychology.    There are several different analytical approaches/perspectives in terms of which social psychologists attempt to explain how and why individuals behave in whichever way that they may actually behave in their various social-cultural contexts. However, there are eight major analytical approaches/perspectives which a majority of social psychologists often adopt in analyzing and explaining the concrete or empirical behaviours of individuals in their various groups, organizations, communities, or societies, as follows:-

(a)    the "Behaviourist" (or stimulus-response) perspective;
(b)    the psychoanalytic perspective;
(c)    the "Symbolic Interactionist" perspective;

(d)     the "Gestalt" perspective;

(e)     the "Field" perspective;

(f)     the "cognitive" perspective;

(g)     the "Dramaturgical" perspective; and

(h)     the "Social Exchange" perspective.

Again, I will not be able to delve into the specific details of each of these different analytical perspectives/ approaches of social psychology in this present essay, largely because of space and time constraints[3]. However, it should suffice it for me to only mention here that it is by using any one of these eight theoretical perspectives that social psychologists are able to describe, explain, and/or predict, in a relatively systematic and intelligible manner, the <u>causes</u> and <u>effects</u> of both the observed and observable substantive empirical facts, events, issues, and problems of social psychology.

## (3)     The Relationship Between the Research Methods and Theories of Psychology

On the whole, the two major component parts of the science of social psychology - namely, "research methodology" and "theoretical analysis" theoretical, analysis" - are very much complementary to each other; for the former furnishes the various concrete empirical facts which form the very unique and indispensable bases for virtually all scientific analyses and explanations, while the latter furnishes the descriptions, explanations, and predictions about the empirical facts. Without theory, empirical facts are disjointed and incoherent; while without concrete empirical facts, any theoretical analysis is

---

[3]     I have also presented and discussed the specific details about each of these eight analytical perspectives a separate essay titled "The Models of Social Man in Social Psychology" (1983). That essay may also be made available by special request to me. Interested students may also consult Chapter One in <u>Social Psychology,</u> by L.S. Wrightsman.

invariably a vague and meaningless speculation that is largely unrelated to the concrete or real world.

## SOCIAL PSYCHOLOGY AS AN ACADEMIC DISCIPLINE AND A PRACTICAL PROFESSION

Social psychology is not only an <u>academic</u> discipline; it is also a practical <u>profession.</u> When we say that any field of learning is an <u>academic</u> discipline, we refer to (1) the premises on which the men in the field rest their work, (2) the ideas and currents of thought which unite or separate them, (3) the characteristic styles of reasoning or argument which they use, (4) the types of data considered, the ways in which they are collected, (5) and the manner In which they are analyzed and disseminated. Whereas, when we speak of a <u>profession,</u> we refer mainly to such things as (1) the practical uses or applications of a body of knowledge - for example, whether to teach or heal; (2) the context in which the discipline is used, whether in public or private, with large groups or face to face with one individual; (3) the way in which those concerned with a given realm make their living; (4) how they are related to their "client", to one another, and to the larger society, (5) how much freedom and autonomy they enjoy; and (6) how well or poorly organized they are. Both the substantive Intellectual nature and practice of a discipline determine both the nature of its **academic** and **professional** enterprises at any particular place and time.

## TRAINING TO BECOME A SOCIAL PSYCHOLOGIST

A social psychologist is any person who has acquired, by learning and writing, the skill or ability of perceiving, identifying describing, explaining, and predicting how and why the thoughts, feelings, and actions of Individuals are influenced by the perceived, imagined, or implied thoughts, feelings, and actions of others. This skill, of social psychology, is acquired mostly through receiving formal training in advanced educational institutions, such as the Universities and allied institutions. People mostly train to become social psychologists in departments of social psychology, sociology, or psychology. In the case of receiving the training in departments of psychology or sociology, the person learns and earns a degree in either psychology or sociology, with a major in social psychology.

Any person who has earned up to a B.Sc. or a higher degree in social psychology is a qualified social psychologist. A person who earned a B.Sc. degree in Sociology or Psychology, with a major in social psychology is also a qualified social psychologist. A person who has earned a B.Sc. degree in sociology or psychology, and merely took a few social psychology courses, is not, strictly speaking, a well trained or qualified social psychologist.

As I had earlier Indicated, there are not yet full-fledged departments of social psychology in Nigeria. However, social psychology courses are offered in the Departments of Sociology, and the Departments of Psychology, in several of the universities in the country, such as in Uniben, Unilag, Abu, Unibadan, etc. Nevertheless, most of the qualified social psychologists in the country at the moment obtained their trainings and qualifications from overseas universities, poly-technics, and the like.

## THE CAREERS FOR SOCIAL PSYCHOLOGISTS

What kinds of jobs is the qualification in social psychology best suited? What kinds of jobs do most qualified social psychologists actually do as a career or profession?

The jobs which a qualified social psychologist is best suited to do include - (1) teaching social psychology in the Various educational institutions which offer social psychology courses;

(2) doing **social-work** in government ministries of social welfare and/or community development, in hospitals, etc; (3) working in personnel management departments in industries, and "other organizations; and (4) working as private consultants in **human relations** matters.

On the whole, the teaching profession absorbs by a largest number of the country's qualified social psychologists. Approximately three quarters of those holding advanced degrees (e.g., M.A./M.Sc., or Ph.D.) in social psychology teach the discipline in the universities and allied educational institutions.

The development of social psychology in Nigerian universities is characterized by the following facts: it is a new comer to the academic scene; its bearers could not point to a well established and venerable intellectual tradition, it is still obscure and hardly known about except in the academic scene. In fact, at present social psychology does not have any independent existence and identity in the country, but rather it exists as a branch of either sociology or psychology.

# SECTION (E)
# THE USES, APPLICATIONS, AND RELEVANCE OF SOCIAL PSYCHOLOGY

One may ask: "Of what use is social psychology?" Or, "Why should any person bother to study social psychology at all?"

There are many different cogent reasons why social psychology should be studied by as many different people as possible. All of such reasons hinge upon and revolve around the important fact that some of the most difficult and perplexing problems and challenges which confront every single individual human being, group, organization, community, or society across the whole world consist of exactly how human beings should deal with, relate to, interact with, or behave towards the very numerous and varied assortment of people - such as fellow tribes peoples, country people, family members, enemies, friends, co-workers, superiors, colleagues, subordinates, strangers, etc - whom they must come across every now and then throughout their life times. On the whole, social psychology - as both a pure and an applied social science - furnishes the people, who are lucky enough to be able to study and understand it properly, with relatively systematic and reliable bodies of "scientific knowledge" about the different ways and manners in which various individuals behave in their various groups, organizations, communities, or societies. When such scientific knowledge is applied in the course of our actually dealing with or relating to one another in either private, or public, or official situations, such scientific social psychological knowledge would definitely enable us to accomplish such interactions much more effectively and beneficially, than if we had not had the invaluable opportunity of studying and knowing anything about social psychology at all.

Social psychologists study and build up their various theories - e.g. theories of motivations role - playing, learning, etc - which show the various ways and manners in which various individuals behave in their various groups, organizations, communities or societies. All of the different sets of "systematic and basic scientific knowledge" about how various individuals behave in their various social and cultural settings, which social psychologists have very painstakingly accumulated over the past several years (and which they are still producing) can be beneficially used or applied to control the behaviour of people in our every day social life in <u>five</u> major way, as follows:-

(1) To help in organizing any group work effectively;
(2) To help an developing individual skills and potentialities effectively;
(3) To help in reducing the rates and seventy of social conflicts, stresses, and strains very effectively.
(4) To help people to determine and control, their total social, cultural, and psychological environments effectively; and
(5) To help in enlightening people about some of the important scientific discoveries which social psychologists have acquired about human behaviour from time to time.

## SUMMARY, CONCLUSION AND RECOMMENDATIONS

In sum, I have endeavoured to show as accurately and as clearly as the available intellectual resources at my disposal at present could permit me to do in this present essay that social psychology is one of the social or human behavioural science subjects. It was first developed in the late 19th century and early 20th century in both Western Europe and North America by social scientists such as J.M. Baldwin, C.H. Cooley, G.H. Mead, Gustave Le Bon, Sigmund Freud, and Floyd Allport.

In the contemporary times, Social Psychology is now taught and learnt in numerous universities and other educational establishments

It fills the major gap that was created by both sociology and psychology in their overly one-sided rendition of man's basic behavioural nature.

For example, sociology largely focuses upon the distinctive social properties of the attitudes and behaviours of individuals/groups/organizations/ communities/societies in themselves. It does not focus extensively or sufficiently on the relatively distinctive individualistic characteristics of the behaviour and related mental processes which are the building blocks of all social systems. Sociology emphasizes that man is completely a product of his society, and that his attitudes and behaviour are predominantly "social". That is, that the attitudes and behaviours of Individuals are a replica or an adjunct of the social attributes of their society. Modern psychological studies, notably by the Freudian Psychoanalysts argue otherwise.

On the other hand, psychology largely focuses on the relatively distinctive nature of the individualistic characteristics of human behaviour and mental processes. It does not focus extensively on the various possible way and manners in which the individual's social and cultural environment exert certain significant influences upon his various attitudes and behaviours. Psychology largely emphasizes the extent to which the biological and mental attributes of organisms (including humans) determine Individual behaviour and mental processes.

In contrast to both sociology and psychology, social psychology mainly focuses upon the social and cultural dimensions of the attitudes and behaviours of individuals. It does so by simultaneously focusing and placing emphasis upon both the "social-cultural", as well as the "psychological/ individualistic" elements in any form of human behaviour, and/or in any form of social interaction. Consequently, social psychology occupies a strategic and valuable eclectic position vis-a-vis psychology and sociology (plus anthropology). In particular, social psychology straddles and integrates several very important elements of sociology, anthropology and psychology together, by virtue of its specialization upon the study of the various social positions which individuals occupy, and the various "social roles" that are attached to those social positions that individuals also act out in their everyday lives.

In short, and very importantly, social psychology is the only social or behavioural science subject that is mainly preoccupied in studying **the various social causes and effects of the various ways and manners in which individual human beings deal with, relate to, or behave towards one another in various social systems, such as groups, organizations, communities, or the larger society as a whole, at any particular point in time.** Social psychology, like sociology and psychology, is also a social/behavioural science. As a social science, social psychology uses relatively standardized scientific research methods and theoretical/analytical perspectives, which its various practitioners employ in studying the attitudes and behaviour of individuals in society. The uses of such standardized research methods and analytical perspectives in social psychology (and also in any other science subject) serve several positive functions, including the fact that they help to ensure that the various sets of specialized information which social psychologists produce from time and from place to place are actually objective, systematic, testable, accurate, and reliable to a great extent.

Lastly, but certainly not the least, the various scientific information which social psychologists produce about the various attitudes and behaviours of individuals are used by different people for different purposes including how to control criminal and delinquent behaviour, how to improve the motivations of individuals, leadership styles and other forms of individual behaviours in various groups and organizations.

# CHAPTER TWO

# SOCIALIZATION AND PERSONALITY DEVELOPMENT

## SECTION (A)

## INTRODUCTION

From the point of view of psychology and other behavioural sciences, every individual human being has his or her own personality. The personality of each person consists of the totality of the physical and mental facilities, and the attitudes and behaviour patterns of the person. The human personality is not created by nature. That is, individuals are not born with their personalities. But rather each person's personality is gradually "moulded" throughout the life span of the individual by the process of dynamic interaction between the individual and various social and cultural forces of society that is called socialization. During socialization, the agents of socialization (e.g. parents, teachers, employers, friends, etc.) teach different aspects of culture (e.g. discipline, aspirations, identities, roles, and skills), while the individual learns and acquires his personality (which comprises his behaviour patterns), which will enable him to engage in socially acceptable and rewarding behaviours throughout his life time. There are different types and results of the process of socialization. But invariably, good and effective socialization produces good personality types, while bad and defective socialization produces bad and defective personality types. The processes of socialization and personality development occur throughout each person's life time.

## SECTION (B)
## DEFINITION OF SOCIALIZATION AND PERSONALITY

### Definitions of Socialization

There are many different acceptable or reliable definitions of socialization in the literature of modern sociology and social psychology, such as the following ones:-

(a)     American sociologist Bruce J. Cohen, defined the concept of "socialization" in his textbook titled Introduction to Sociology (1979: page 45) as follows:

Socialization is the process through which a human begins to learn the way of life of his or her society, acquire a personality, and develop the capacity to function both as an individual and as a member of the group.

(b)     Three contemporary American Social Psychologists Lawrence J. Severy, John D. Brigham, and Barry R. Schlenker defined socialization in their textbook titled A Contemporary Introduction to Social Psychology (1976: page 141), as follows:

The process of bringing an individual's social behaviour into line with the culture is known as Socialization.

(c)     American social psychologist Edwin P. Hollander defined "Socialization" in his textbook titled. Principles and Method of Social Psychology (third Edition, 1976; page 99), as follows:

An infant is born with the potential for a wide variety of behaviours. Which ones are developed depends upon the operation of a complex of factors, especially interaction with others. Growing up in a human society, the child learns to restrain certain impulses and to adopt the characteristics and values of the people in a particular social environment. This process is called <u>Socialization.</u> It varies greatly from place to place and from person to person, which allows for many similarities as well as differences among individuals.

The most vital feature of socialization is acquiring distinctive human qualities that can only come from contact with other humans. Language, attitudes, a sense of social organization, and moral conduct, are some of those qualities. They are impressed upon us from the earliest years of development onward, and therefore a great deal of learning must occur in early life.

Socialization is part of a life-going process of adjustment. In life there are several goals which require fulfilment: gaming the necessities for physical well-being; meeting the demands of other people in the social environment; and achieving one's own potentialities. These provide the essential framework for adjustment. (Page 99).

Socialization means learning the ways of a given society or group well enough to be able to function according to its rules. More than behaviour alone, it involves taking on socially approved values and attitudes. (Page 119).

In short, socialization operates to bring about socially approved regularities in behaviour, values, and attitudes. (Page 120).

(d)     Indian Social Psychologist, B. Kuppuswamy, define "Socialization" in his textbook titled <u>Elements of Social Psychology</u> (1979: page 39), as follows:

Socialization is the interactional process by which the child's behaviour is modified to conform to the expectations held by the members of the group to which he belongs. It also includes the process by which an adult acquires the behaviour appropriate to the expectation associated with a new position in a group, an organization, or society at large.

(e)     Two Nigerian Sociologists Onigu Otite and William Ogionwo defined "Socialization" in their textbook titled. <u>An Introduction to Sociologically Studies</u> (1981: page 223), as follows:

In broad terms, socialization is the process by which beings who are biologically human become socially human. It is the process by which man acquires his social behaviour patterns.

(f)     Two American Sociologists Leonard Broom and Philip Selznick defined "Socialization" in their textbook titled. <u>Sociology:</u> A Text With Adapted Readings (Fifth Edition, 1973: page 91), as follows:

From the perspective of society, socialization is the process of fitting new individuals into an organized way of life and an established cultural tradition. Socialization begins very early and is a lifelong process. As the individual participates in new social forms and institutions, he learns new disciplines and develops new values.

From the perspective of the individual, socialization is the process by which the human animal becomes a human being and acquires a self. Through interaction with others in a cultural context, the individual gains an identity, takes an ideals, values, and aspirations, and under favourable circumstances becomes capable of self-realizing activity. Socialization may fail in these respects; it may constrain and inhabit personal development. Nevertheless it is the indispensable condition for self-awareness and for the formation of individual identity. Thus socialization represents two complementary processes: the transmission of a social and cultural heritage and the development of personality.

## Definitions of Human Personality

There are also several plausible definitions of the concepts of "human personality", or simply "personality" in the literatures of sociology psychology and social psychology, such as follows:

(a)    American sociologist Bruce J. Cohen defined "personality" in his aforementioned book (page 49) as follows:

Personality refers to all of the characteristics and traits which are representative of a person's behaviour. Included are patterns of thoughts and feelings, self-conception, attitudes, mentality, and overt habits.

(b)     American Social Psychologist Edwin P. Hollander defined the "Human Personality" in his already above-mentioned textbook (page 324), as follows:
     (An individual's personality is) the sum total of an individual's characteristics which make him or her unique.

(c)     Three American Social Psychologists Paul F. Second, Carl W. Backman, and David R. Slavitt defined "Human Personality" in their textbook title, Understanding Social Life: An Introduction to Social Psychology (1976: page 5), as follows:
     Analysis in terms of personality considers properties of individuals such as attitudes, traits, feelings, habits, needs, and motives, as well as the way in which the individual conceives of himself and the world around him. Such analysis emphasizes the differences between one individual and another, and attempts to identify the distinguishing characteristics of a person, whether they be attitudes, motives, habits, or whatever.

(d)     While the American Psychologist Charles G. Morris defined "Personality" in his textbook titled Psychology: An Introduction Sixth Edition (1988: page 458) as follows:-
     Personality is a person's unique pattern of thoughts, feelings, and behaviours that persist over time and situation.

**Summary of the Definitions of Socialization and Personality**

We have deliberately quoted <u>six</u> definitions of "socialization" and <u>four</u> definitions of "personality" from standard textbooks in psychology, social psychology and sociology to enable the reader to see and appreciate both the common and varied elements of socialization and personality which the experts in the three disciplines recognize and emphasize. Therefore we strongly urge the reader to read all the ten definitions carefully, and summarize both the <u>similarities</u> and <u>differences</u> in the <u>definitions</u> of "socialization" on the one hand, and those of "personality" on the other hand. That exercise when completed, will enable the reader to acquire a versatile and reliable knowledge and understanding of these two key concepts in this chapter.

# SECTION C
# THE OBJECTIVES OF SOCIALIZATION

All the six definitions of socialization quoted above, recognize that socialization benefits the individual by moulding his personality. However, Broom and Selznick went further in their definition and pointed out that socialization also benefits society. Thus, Broom and Selznick analyzed the goals of socialization from two perspectives: the society and the individual. According to them "From the perspective of society, socialization is the process of fitting new individuals into an organized way of life and an established cultural tradition; "while from "the perspective of the individual, socialization is the process by which the human animal becomes a human being and acquires a self."

We, in this text, strongly endorse Broom and Selznicks conceptualization of socialization's dual goals. We shall point out the merits of recognizing that socialization benefit is both society and the individual, and the demerits of recognizing or emphasizing only the individuals gains from socialization when examine the different types of personalities that emerge from different forms of socialization later in this chapter.

**The Social Objectives of Socialization**
From the standpoint of society, Socialization aims to achieve the following <u>four</u> major objectives, among several other possible ones:

(1)    To transmit a society's cultural values, knowledge, and norms to now generations and strangers, so that they could behave in social predictable and acceptable ways.

(2)    To ensure uniformity or standardization in social behaviour and thereby fit individuals properly into organized ways of life in society.

(3)     To maintain harmony, stability, and continuity in cherished aspects of social institutions and patterns of social organization in society.

(4)     To bring about desired social changes in society smoothly and successfully.


## The Psychological Objectives of Socialization

From the standpoint of the individual, socialization, according to Broom and Selznick (1973:pp94-95) attempts to accomplish the following <u>five</u> major goals:

1.      Socialization inculcates basic <u>disciples,</u> ranging form the relatively simple toilet habits to the very intricate methods of science. Undisciplined behaviour is prompted by impulse. It ignores future consequences and satisfactions in favour of immediate and perhaps transitory gratifications. Discipline behaviour restricts immediate gratifications either by postponing, foregoing, or modifying them, sometimes to gain social approval, sometimes for the sake of a future goal.

Disciplines can reach so deep as to modify physiological responses. Many people wake up early whether they want to or not, and individuals often become physically incapable or performing socially prohibited acts. A person may become ill after eating tabooed food; the sexual impulse may be so restricted by social prohibitions that impotence results. While disciplines are necessary for social order and individual fulfilment, they may encapsulate the individual within provincial groups and narrow perspective or deter his/her self realization.

2.      Socialization Instills <u>aspirations.</u> Because disciplines are often arduous and unrewarding in themselves, they are

best sustained when the individual sees them as means to realizing goals. Every society instills in each of its members a variety of aspirations corresponding to the status the individual will occupy in society by virtue of his/her sex, age, family, and group affiliation. For example, in pre-industrial society, a cobbler would try to instill in his son the desire to be a good cobbler on week days, a faithful attendant at Sunday services, a good trencherman on feast days, and a leader of the cobblers' guild in his mature years. His daughter would have been inspired with aspirations to be a pious churchgoer, a diligent and capable house keeper, and a devoted wife and mother. This illustration is a reminder that, especially in traditional societies, socialization has the aim of restricting aspirations as much as instilling them.

3.  Socialization provides individuals with <u>identities,</u> largely through the aspiration it encourages or discourages. Many upper - class young Englishmen were once taught upper - class etiquette by their valets. But knowledge of upper - class manners could not make the "gentle man's gentleman" upper class either his own eyes or in the eyes of others. Although he knew how to act like a gentleman perhaps better than the gentlemen, he did not have the identity of a gentleman. In contemporary industrial society, aspirations are less securely fixed than in preliterate and traditional society. One consequence appears to be a weaker sense of identity among young people. In modern society, a sense of personal identity seems to be achieved later in life than in past eras; individuals now have more options, and socialization is less closely dependent on such factors as sex, ethnic identities, and family status.

4.  Socialization teaches <u>social roles</u> and their supporting attitudes. Social roles, aspirations identities, and disciplines are interrelated. For example, the catholic priest-hood is a religious and occupational aspiration, a discipline in emotional restraint and celibacy, a personal identity and a social role.

    Traditionally, the priest is encouraged to assume attitudes, or respect towards his superiors and sympathy and compassion towards his parishioners, even when these attitudes do not reflect his personal feelings at the moment. This does not imply that supporting attitudes are taught as mere external manner. An effective social institution instills in the individuals it trains a set of inwardly felt sentiments and emotions. It is a sign of institutional and organizational weakness when socialization is superficial and social roles are mechanical performances.

5.  Socialization teachers <u>skills.</u> Only by acquiring skills can individuals fit into a society. In simply societies traditional practices are handed down from generation to generation and are usually learned by imitation and practice in the course of everyday life. In societies with advanced technology, inculcating the abstract skills of literacy through formal education is a central task of socialization. The individual who lacks appropriate skill is economically unproductive relegated to the margins of society and likely to feel alienated from both the society and himself. In other words, formal education has become a necessary condition for effective socialization

into the existing social order of any modern society, e.g. Nigeria.

In sum, it is largely by the acquisition of all of these five as well as other related psychological elements of behaviours - through learning from socialization agencies - that each typical individual human infant developments into a more or less adequate member of his/her society. In other words, this development is largely a process of learning. "Socialization" is <u>learning</u> that enables the learner to perform social roles. Thus, in the final analysis, it is <u>culture</u> that is learned in socialization, because all the different aspects of social behaviour that the ind-acquires are properties of culture.

## INTERNALIZED OBJECTS

At this junction, it is necessary that we should have some understanding of the important fact that there is a fundamental distinction or difference between any human being's <u>infant's organism</u> on the one hand, and the <u>adult's personality,</u> which emerges through socialization, on the other hand. We cannot speak of the infant's "personality" in a strict sense, because it does not actually have any. For, a human personality is, in one respect, a <u>complex inner system</u> which "represents" <u>the outer</u> world. It largely depends on a consciousness of self as against the outer world of objects - be they animate or inanimate ones. The adult's inner construction of the outer world will not be necessarily accurate in all details; yet even a psychotic's personality reflects, however imperfectly, some of the features of objective reality. But on the other hand, for the newborn infant, there is no objective reality, as such - that is, there is no space, no time, no causality, etc. The mother's breast, a bottle, a rattle, etc, are not things in themselves, which are existing independently of the infant's own existence. But rather, to him, they are somewhat capricious comings and goings of sensory images, images not perceived as images of things nor distinguished, presumably, from the acts of sucking, seeing, hearing, touching, and the like. That is to say that at first the infant does not distinguish between his own perceiving and the things perceived. Having as yet no self consciousness, he simply acts as if the whole world which impinges upon him were particularly and parcel of himself.

What is an "internalized object"? Psychologically, it simply means any individual's "cognitive map" of any external object (or class of objects). The object itself is "external" in the sense that it has a socially agreed - upon objective reality or existence - i.e. it is not merely a figment of any one's imagination. The term "cognitive map" is quite appropriate in the context of socialization/personality study, because, like an ordinary map, the internalized object is a symbol (i.e. "a representation") of something else. As a map of Kiagbodo Township in the Burutu Local Government Council Area of State "represents" the various buildings and streets of the (author's home) town, that is also how any internalized object also represents any corresponding external object - which may, of course, be a person, a thing, or a class of persons or things. In short, all the things which each individual human being has learnt and acquired during socialization, such as all of the above - mentioned (5) major behavioural traits, represent the "internalized objects" that make up his personality. In that way, each adult individual is able to draw upon them in order for him to use them from time to time for ganging the various ways and manners in which he would relate/react to the concrete aspects of the external world which correspond to his "internalized objects". Each human being gradually builds up his total set of internalized objects from one stage of socialization to another.

The total set of one's "internalized objects" makes up one's total set of knowledge at any particular period of time during his life-span. Therefore, the greater the quantity and the quality of one's internalized objects, the greater is one's total stock of knowledge at any given point in time, and vice-versa. Since knowledge is power, it follows that the greater the amount of knowledge one acquires, the more powerful one is in society, and vice-versa.

## THE SELF

As we had also earlier indicated above, the infant at birth does not have any self-consciousness, as such. But at the same time that he is building up internalized objects which correspond to other people and to things, he is also building up a concept of himself as an object. The concept of "self" technically refers to the one's internalized objects which represent one's own "personality". Thus, one's concept of "self" includes one's own conception of one's discipline, aspirations, identities, roles, skills, etc; one's own evaluation of those and other aspects of one's personality, and certain feelings of pride, shame, and self-respect, any one of which can be activated under certain circumstances. One's construction of one's self and one's construction of one's other internalized objects always invariably go on together. Most importantly, for our primary objective in this present course/ lecture of trying to know exactly how we can identify and understand the distinctive nature and characteristics of any one human personality, we should note right away at this juncture that any one individual who is incapable of distinguishing himself/herself as a separate social behavioural entity, cannot also adequately distinguish other people and things as separate entities. Such are the individuals who are invariably "problematic" or "abnormal" adults. That is because, like infants they still think or regard the whole of the world which surrounds them as their own individual selves write large. That is an abnormal way of thinking about one's self vis-a-vis the rest of the world, because in any such an abnormal person's attempt to act for other people, he/she would invariably encounter serious clashes or conflicts with such other people.

In the final analysis, therefore, the sum total of all of the above mentioned <u>five</u> major behavioural traits, plus any other ones, which any one individual has learnt/acquired during socialization represent the internalized objects which makes up his/her "self", which in turn represents the "psychological core" of his/her total personality structure. Consequently, any adult individual can be said to have accomplished the psychological aims of socialization, if his/her learning during socialization has actually left some relatively distinctive and significant "traces" of "cognitive maps", in his/her brain or mind, which make up both his/her "self" and "personality", which also represents the predominant behavioural traits which he/she would subsequently act out from adult-age through old-age, and which will

also represent his/her own distinctive "personal identity" vis-a-vis all other human beings - including even one's own relatives, children, friends, enemies, etc.

# SECTION D
# THE BIOLOGICAL BASIS OF SOCIALIZATION

Human beings possess certain fundamental biological factors which make socialization both possible and necessary. There are <u>three</u> major ones, as follows: (1) Human inter-dependency; (2) Capacity to learn; and (3) Capacity to act.

## 1.     Human Inter-dependency:-

Human beings cannot meet their wants and needs individually, by themselves alone, but instead they <u>depend</u> completely upon social interaction and mutual exchanges with one another to enable them to obtain all of their several different existential needs. The fact of the inevitability of human inter-dependency is best exemplified by the way in which infants, children, aged, and invalidated people conspicuously and completely depend upon their significant others for their everyday wants and needs. Human inter-dependency therefore necessitates that all human beings are subjected to one form or the other of some extensive and even gruelling processes of socialization where they learn what to do in order to get what they want and need out of life.

## 2.     Capacity of Learn:-

The socialization process of teaching and learning is made biologically possible by virtue of the fact that human beings have the capacity to learn. Human beings' capacity to learn is due to their possession of a large and plastic brain. The largeness of the human brain makes it possible for the individual to acquire, retain and utilize language. This attribute is particularly important in socialization because the teaching and learning process in socialization predominantly entails linguistic communication. On the other hand, the plastic nature

72

of the human brain makes it possible for human beings to learn and adapt to new things, living conditions, and different socialization situations.

### 3.    Capacity to Act:-

As a corollary of the previous factor, the socialization process is also made biologically possible by human beings' capacity to act. Human beings' capacity to act is due to the peculiar physical structure of the human body. For example, the <u>upright posture of the human body</u> frees the hands and legs to manipulate tools. Furthermore, <u>the prehensile structure of the human hands,</u> and the <u>opposable nature of the thumbs</u> are also important for the same reason.

Despite the importance of the above and any other biological factors in making the socialization of human beings both possible and necessary, it is also necessary to note that all basic biological givens merely underlie the behavioural phenomena which eventually emerge there-from. That is, <u>heredity</u> only supplies the needs, potential capabilities, and limitations of the human organism. Even the basic drives of hunger and sex are general and undirected. It is under socialization that all of them are reshaped, through cultural definitions, into socially approved channels. Thus, to the extent that different ways of eating, behaving and living vary from one community to another, to that extent we must recognise the special importance of socialization in human development and survival.

# SECTION E
## AGENCIES OF SOCIALIZATION

The basic disciplines, aspirations, identities, social roles and skills which are taught and learned during socialization are parts and parcels of the cultural heritage of society. The teaching and learning processes which make up socialization involves two complementary functionaries, namely; <u>Socialization agents and individuals:</u> The former perform the role of teaching while the latter learn.

It's assumed that the agencies of socialization are already proficient in the values and behavioural patterns of the society. They are therefore the custodians and transmitters of the cultural heritage of that society. Although, there are some significant variations in the types of socialization agencies which operate from one society to another, there are nevertheless certain fairly standard and universal ones in all over the modem western and capitalist world with Nigeria inclusive. These are as follows:-

(1)     The family
(2)     The peer group
(3)     The school
(4)     The mass media
(5)     The work place, and
(6)     Total institutions


1.     **The Family:** In most societies, the family is the initial and most important of the agencies of socialization. Although its structure varies considerably across cultures, responsibility for the care of the young is assigned. The family does not tend merely to the physical needs of the infant. It also assumes the task of teaching moral rules, disciplines such as toilet habits and the norms of

propriety and also social skills. The family also continues to be a major force in the shaping of the personalities of individuals through old age and death. It instills aspirations and identities, in the individual, hence most of the important connections that individuals have in later life tend to be derived from their family backgrounds. The popular saying that 'charity begins at home', clearly exemplifies the special importance of the <u>role</u> of the family in the total socialization scheme.

2.     **The Peer Group**:- The peer group complements the family in the socialization of the individual. Initially, the peer-group socializes the child into the world of the young and adolescents, and into the particular values that these age groups hold. In these early contacts with peers, the individual learns to modify his behaviour so that he is accepted by others, and he learns to acknowledge the impersonal authority of the group as well as the personal authority of parents. But the individual continues to learn from peer groups for as long as he lives, because in the modern life, each individual will find many roles which will require his working with his peers or colleagues, e.g. as a pupil. Boys Scout, Student Secretary, Manager, Housewife, Salesman, and retired persons.

3.     **The School:-** By the term "school" is simply meant all the different levels of formal educational institutions which characterize any modern society. They range from kindergarten, primary school, secondary or grammar school, technical or commercial schools, teachers training school, polytechnics, up to university and beyond.

The major socialization function of the school is to impact technical and professionally oriented academic <u>skills</u> and <u>disciplines</u> to individuals. That is, it is largely through schools that modern individuals learn and acquire certain specific professional skills and their associated professional codes of conducts. These skills and disciplines enable them to take up technical roles as employers or employees in several fields ranging from engineering, nursing, teaching, banking, law enforcement, adjudication, to politics. The increased complexity and technicality of modern professional skills make a long period of formal education inevitable so that individuals can acquire higher professional skills and gain greater proficiency in their jobs.

4.    **The Mass Media:-** The term "mass media" refers to all the different media of mass communications which predominantly characterize modern societies. It includes news papers, journals, radios land televisions. Industrialization, urbanization and modernization have created the societal conditions which necessitate the development of mass communications as well as the pervasive and wide-spread influences which they exert in modern societies.

Mass communication comprises the institutions and techniques by which specialized social groups employ the technological devices of the mass media to disseminate information to large heterogeneous and widely dispersed audiences. The major function which the mass media plays in socialization is that it socializes individuals into the broad social, economic, political, religious, and other aspects of the culture and value system of any society e.g., Nigeria.

It does so by disseminating relatively standardized, structured, organised, comprehensive, authentic and functional news and public opinions about government laws, policies, educational and occupational opportunities, politics, development ideological fermentations, and other general problems, events and issues in and about the society both for the information as well as for the practical utilization of various individuals, interest groups, organizations, and communities.

Consequently, the mass media provides individuals with the requisite knowledge and concrete interaction contexts which enables them to participate in public life, keep abreast with developments around them and have some adequate sense of belonging to their society.

5. **The work place:-** The term workplace refers to all the different occupational groups which all of a society's different adult individuals belong to and interact in for the purpose of earning their means of livelihood. In these contexts, individuals apply their acquired technical and professional skills and disciplines towards acting out certain particular types of roles which are attached to their various status as employers or employees. These work places exert a great deal of different kinds of potent influences on the personalities of the various individuals in the sense that their evaluations of them determine their values and the payoffs of the different academic and professional trainings, which they had received from their previous educational backgrounds. These rewards

would in turn determine the concrete emotional and material rewards which they will get out of their working experiences to enable them live the appropriate style of life, which is commensurate with their acquired socio-economic statuses as well as their values, identities and aspirations. In workplaces individuals invariably modify and/or augment many of their previously values, identities, and aspirations. In fact the workplace is the dominant socialization agency during much of the adult life of most human beings.

6.    **Total Institution:-** The term "total institution" is used in socialization to refer to such quasi-communal social groups and organizations like the prisons, orphanages, sanitaria, asylums, remand homes, and the special hospitals for the mentally ill people in the society. The major function which they perform in socialization is the resocialization of the failures and other casualties of socialization, such as criminals, juvenile delinquents, mad people, orphans, invalids, the aged, etc.

Total institutions are either correctional, punitive, or both in their orientations towards socialization.

# SECTION F
# MODES OF SOCIAL LEARNING

The specific mechanisms of socialization are only now beginning to be understood. At least <u>four</u> different modes of social learning may be identified, as follows:- Conditioning, identify- taking, Modelling-after, and problem-solving.

1.   **Conditioning:-** Much of learning is based on the principle of association. An organism is said to be conditioned when a response pattern is build into the organism as a result of environmental stimuli. Normally, conditioning requires repetitive associations of stimulus and response, but a response pattern may result from a single significant experience.

   Classical conditioning associated with the name of Ivan Pavlov, and John B. Watson, builds upon an existing stimulus - response patterns. In dogs (and people) the connection between salivation and food testing is an unlearned or unconditioned response. The salivation response can be conditioned, however, by introducing another stimulus that is maintained, for a time, in constant association with the original stimulus. Thus if a bell is sounded repeatedly when food is presented to a dog, the dog learns to salivate in response to the bell. This response is now a conditioned response.

   Thus classical conditioning varies the stimulus while the response remains constant. The dog continues to salivate but the stimulus is different. Similarly, it has recently been shown that ten-day-old babies can "learn" to blink at the sound of a tone if the sound is systematically paired with a puff of air directed at the baby's eyes.

In contrast, operant or instrumental conditioning tries to control the response. Certain animal responses, such as turning left in a rat maze, can be effectively extinguished if they are systematically followed by the infliction of pain, e.g, from an electric shock; others, such as taking a right turn in a maze, can be made routine or habitual by rewarding the animal with food, or even by withholding the electric shock that would otherwise be forth coming. By using operant conditioning, animals have been induced to perform in uncharacteristic ways for example, seals to blow horns, dogs to dance, chimpanzees to do simple arithmetic.

The word operant suggests work done, an effect produced. Hence behaviour is operant when it is guided by an anticipated result, e.g, moving to avoid a blow, or opening the deer to walk outside. These example point to an important distinction. "Operant conditioning" is the creation of a built in response pattern as a result of systematic reinforcement, including negative reinforcement. Moving out of the way to avoid or blow is often a pattern established by operant conditioning. On the other hand, a singe means and action, such as opening a door, is an example of operant or instrumental learning, but not necessarily of conditioning.

Conditioning offers a valid if limited perspective on social learning. Classical conditioning demonstrated the feasibility of increasing the repertory of stimuli to which an animal will respond; Pavlov's dogs learned to salivate at the sound of a bell as well as at the sight of food. Without this ability to learn to respond to ever-larger classes of stimuli, human learning would be impossible. Similarly, without the capacity for operant conditioning, human beings would not be able to transcend their biological limitations. Perhaps the most important contribution of conditioning to socialization is that conditioning builds a bridge from man as a biological organism to man as a social being. Through classical conditioning, infant and young child learn to respond to social or man-made stimuli e.g. with smiles to the nursing bottle, with tears at the sight of bitter testing medicine-just as through operant conditioning they learn to inhibit certain responses and adopt others as habitual.

2.  **Identity-Taking:-** Studies of European and American children show that children only gradually acquire the idea of the stability of objects, the immutability of species, and the unchangeability of biological sex. However, by the time they are five most children correctly identify themselves and others by sex and already behave in the stereotypical ways assigned to men and women by the societies of which they are members. Some experts on socialization believe that sex-typed behaviour emerges largely through operant conditioning. They reason that children first engage in a wide range of behaviours, only gradually learning to inhibit those assigned to the others sex.

   While approval and disapproval, reward and punishment, undoubtedly play a large part in socialization for maleness and female-ness, it is doubtful that conditioning alone accounts for sex differences in behaviour. With the acquisition of language and cognitive skills, the child can hear himself being called a boy or girl, accept the label, learn by observation and report what girls and boys do, and behave accordingly. Without a foundation of conditioning i.e., associating conformity with approval and deviance with disapproval-labelling would be ineffective as a socialization device. Nevertheless, once the basic ground rules have been learned, labelling on the part of others and identity-taking on the part of the individual constitute a process by which traditional social roles are easily transmitted. Throughout life, the individual takes on a number of identities and myself assumes responsibility for learning the "official" role requirements of student, spouse, employee, employer, etc.

3.     **Modelling-After:-** This basically refers to a method of non routine, often emotion-laden form of identity-taking in the selection of an admired, love, or feared figure to model oneself after. Modelling-after appears to be a typical stage in the form of personality and in the development of both personal autonomy and social involvement. By means of a model he himself has chose, the individual gains some independence from his immediate environment and, at the same time, established a unique relation with a selected portion of the social world. The individual acquires a self-chosen identity which he values and which contributes to his self-esteem. Though a model, behaviour acquires meaning and coherence and becomes something more than an instinctive or forced conformity to conventional expectations.

Paradoxically, this form of deep social influences has liberating effect in-so-far as the individual gains from the model of "his own" standards of excellence and criteria of choice. On the other hand, this type of identification can be constraining, especially when it is accompanied by strong dependency feelings. They person may then foreclose his options and inhibit the development of his mil range of potentialities.

4.  **Problem-Solving:-** The mechanisms discussed above are, for the most part, modes of internalisation. They are the ways by which norms values-including deviant normal and deviant values-become part of the individual's personality and establish his characteristic way of responding. But social learning is something more than the mere internalisation of norms and values. It is also learning to participate in co-operative and conflictual activities, to cope with new situations, and to achieve one's goals in a context of opportunity and constraint.

A problem-solving orientation is necessary for effective social participation, especially in a complex and fluid society. Yet such an orientation is often difficult to achieve. Psychological difficulties get in the way as when a person is more interested in 'ego trips' than in "the task at hand." Social norms may also be counter-productive if they become ways of programming conduct in detail rather than providing general frameworks within which effective action can take place.

In this context, problem-solving is not an intellectual operation, like solving a problem in mathematics, but the re-attainment of equilibrium as a result of some action taken to change the environment or oneself. It is applied to a problematic social situation, one that makes the individual uncomfortable, and, which therefore, calls for some painstaking response from him/her.

All distinguished "achievers"- e.g., Kwame Nkrumah, Obafemi Awolowo, Michael Okpara, Audu Bako, Samuel Osaigbovo Ogbemudia, Murtala R. Mohammed, Lateef Jakande, etc - are all very eloquent examples of "problem-solvers" or "action-men". This "problem-solving" approach to social learning and self-actualization requires that the individual must consciously and determinedly adopt and constantly apply very sound cognitive or intellectual, and moral or ethical standards of personal character and behaviour in virtually everything which he/her does in his/her everyday life. In comparison with the other modes of social learning, this "problem-solving" approach is the most effective in ensuring the development of an "adequate ego".

However, it should also be carefully noted that no one single mode of social learning can adequately account for all of socialization. The development of an autonomous cognitive and emotional organization leads the child to resist and transcend conditioning. For example, a child does not have to be repeatedly given to free by a fond ground-parent in order for him to associate the two. With the acquisition of language, he is soon able to understand the idea of reward and punishment and as such does not have to experience them directly. He becomes, capable of controlling his own behaviour.

Perhaps more importantly is the fact that each mode of social learning has its own set of distinctive limitations, and as a result, no single mode can be completely relied upon. Even where conditioning is effective, it may produce maladaptive and dysfunctional response patterns. The very conditioned individual may be at a serious disadvantage in complex societies, in period of social change, or a novel situations that require flexibility. The main limitation of identity-taking is the possibility of great discrepancy between the individual's personality and the identity which he or she takes on. It does not matter much whether children are born with certain temperaments or acquire them during the first few years of life; in either case they are equipped very early with an inner nature that may be seriously frustrated by the stereotypical roles and labels which are assigned to them by society. Modelling-after also has its own characteristic problems; for the person, it is the risk of excessive imitation and dependency; whereas for the society, it may be the possible of glorifying destructive heroes. Finally, problem-solving, since it encourages a political and practical spirit, it may too drastically erodes existing norms and values. Many of the beliefs and practices that bind societies together are high parochial and founded more in myth than in fact. Training in problem-solving is to some extent a process of desocialization for it involves unlearning the easily truths of childhood and criticizing established ways.

## Socialization and Some Major Emergent Types of Basic Social Characters/Human Personalities

From all the foregoing analyses so far, students can clearly see for themselves that through socialization each culture places a distinctive mark upon human personality. Perhaps, the most important point which students must note very carefully in this respect is the fact that every culture can only mould/socialize its various individual members in its own image. A culture which is predominantly replete with beliefs in the powers of witchcraft, witches, wizards and sorcerers, will also largely socialize a majority of its people to believe in and strive to acquire the power of witchcraft, witches, etc. A culture which is dominated by the feelings of "big-manism", will also socialise its individual members to cultivate the habits of swaggering, expanding hollow chests, and acting like big men", even when they do not have any concrete/substantial achievements to their credit. A culture which believes in polygamous marriages, will likewise socialize its members to struggle to "marry" more than one wife (polygamy) or more than one husband (polyandry). A culture which cherishes monogamy and all of its attendant orderly, peaceful, progressive and refined ways of living and rearing children, will also socialize its various men and women to practise monogamy.

# CHAPTER THREE

## THE PSYCHOANALYTIC PERSPECTIVE ON THE NATURE OF THE HUMAN PERSONALITY

### (A)    INTRODUCTION

The objective study of the processes of socialization and personality development was given its initial impetus by the work of Sigmund Freud. He was the pioneer, that is, the first to attempt a comprehensive theory of the structure and dynamics of the human personality, to claim that there was order in the manifold processes of personality development, and to point to the key dimensions that he saw as defining the central problems of socialization in early childhood. The theory and method of studying the personality which Freud discovered is called **Psychoanalysis**.

According to the psychoanalytic perspective, personality development proceeds through a fixed series of stages during the first five years of life. These are decisive years for the adult personality. The stages are based on the primary of "erogenous zones" of the body. An **erogenous zone** is an area of the skin or mucous membrane that, when stimulated, produces pleasurable sensations.

In explaining why individuals behave in whatever ways in which they behave, Freud placed the greatest amount of premium on the role of **unconscious** motives in directing behaviour. Freud compared the human mind to an iceberg. He said that like iceberg, there is a small part of the human mind that represents all that the individual is aware of at any particular point in time and Freud called that part of the mind the individual's **conscious experience**. While the much larger part of individual's mind represents the **unconscious** – a storehouse or reservoir of impulses, passions, and inaccessible memories that affect each individual's thoughts and behaviour.

To understand and appreciate the contributions of the psychoanalytic approach to the nature of the human personality in its proper perspective, we shall discuss it under the following major subheadings: Firstly, we shall examine the basic assumptions of the psychoanalytic perspective. Secondly, we shall analyse Freud's stages of psychological development and their extension by Erick Erikson's ages of man. Thirdly, we shall look at Freud's tripartite division of the structure of the human personality into "Id", "Ego" and "Superego". And fourthly, we shall also examine the psychoanalytic view of human anxiety and the defenses against it.


## (B)    BASIC ASSUMPTIONS

The psychoanalytic perspective is based on a number of fundamental assumptions about human behaviour, as follows:-

### (1) Unconscious Psychological Processes

Slips of the tongue, sudden lapses of memory, and symbolic events in dreams are thought to be due to **psychological processes operating in an area of an individual's psychology outside our conscious awareness** which Freud called the unconscious area of the human mind. Freud developed the ideas of **unconscious, preconscious and conscious** mental activity as portrayed in Figure 1 – 1. Conscious mental activity refers to immediate experience, what you are experiencing right now. Although this experience is most easily accessible, it also comprises the smallest amount of mental life.

The preconscious mental domain includes all those events, thoughts, ideas and memories outside immediate awareness but which are available to you. Thus, although you remember a friend's telephone number or the colour of a sweater, it is preconscious, and not always in your awareness. Finally, the largest domain of mental activity is the unconscious. The unconscious is a vast reservoir of childhood and current memories, fears, hopes, wishes, impulses, and thoughts that are seldom if ever available to one's consciousness. In fact, Freud believed that these thoughts are kept out of awareness by a **censoring** process that protects the person from the threats of unacceptable unconscious wishes or threatening impulses.

Freud was aware that unconscious processes could only be inferred from observable psychological phenomena, and that the unconscious itself could never be directly observed. Furthermore, he believed that unconscious ideas were subject to distortion and unlike conscious ideas often lacked a logical relation to one another. Many of the apparently illogical events in dreams illustrate this quality.

Unlike previous writers who had invoked the concept of unconscious processes, Freud was inclined to give them a primary role as determinants of behaviour. Other writers had suggested that although unconscious processes might exist, they were of secondary importance in the psychological life of the individual. Freud, on the other hand, perhaps because of his unique experiences with hypnosis and neurotic patients, was convinced that unconscious processes played a dominant role in determining behaviour.

**Fig. 1-1:- Relationship between the unconscious, preconscious, and conscious domains of psychological life.**

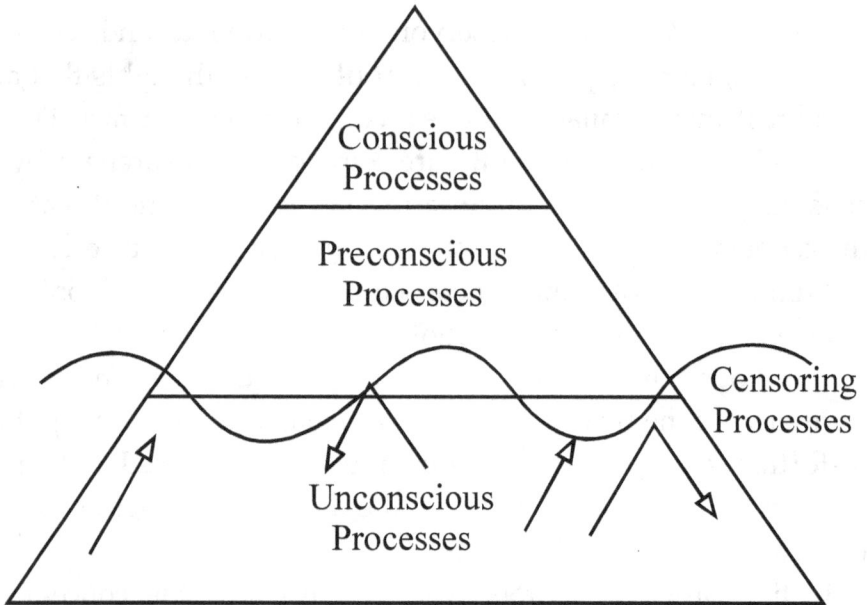

*Source:* Richard H. Price, **Abnormal Behaviour, Perspectives in Conflict**, Second Edition. New York: Holt, Rinehart and Winston, (1978), p. 33.

Thus, from Freud's work comes an understanding of the importance of the unconscious aspect of beliefs, particularly in giving to knowledge significance and order for the person. **In the interpretation of dreams**, Freud described the processes through which ideas can take on multiple meanings, the process in which the mind "displaces" the content of experience unto a chain of reasoning, and the complementary process through which this chain of reasoning and memory is "condensed" during the process of displacement. Thus, "displacement" is the process through which one idea (with negative implications for the person) is replaced with another (less threatening, more acceptable) idea. The second (or third or fourth and so on), less anxiety provoking idea is used to say, obliquely, what could not be said before, directly, simultaneously, various sets of meanings are displaced onto one idea which becomes the condensation of many different meanings or chains or meaning. Freud thus explained, by tracing the interactive processes of condensation and displacement, how "conscious" thought becomes a "code for" the (repressed) unconscious. By unravelling this code, the structure of needs and understanding which motivate a person, the implicit pattern of significance which gives meaning to experience and to action for the person, could be discovered. Much of Freud's explication of the details of these psychological processes – particularly his statements about the importance of instinct or of sexuality, or about the psychology of women – is now either dismissed or the subject or great debate; and much of this questioning has been the result of the comparative work of anthropologists such as Bronislaw Malinowski and Margaret Mead. But the basic skeleton of the workings of the mind and dynamics of the relations between conscious and unconscious, of code and meaning – of the working, in fact, of ideas in human consciousness - is Freud's lasting contribution to the understanding of people.

## (2)    Behaviour is Purposive

For Freud, all behaviour, both neurotic and normal, was seen as motivated or caused. Freud's causal statements about behaviour attempted to describe both the present purposes of the behaviour and its earlier determinants. Thus, symptoms did not simply appear but served a purpose. Often the purpose of symptoms as Freud saw them was to avoid painful memories or thoughts. His sensitivity and perceptiveness as a clinician allowed him to notice the way in which symptoms sometimes had a logic of their own.

## (3)    Conflict of Motives

Freud believed people were continually struggling with conflicts as occurring between opposing motives or drives. For example, he was particularly impressed with the fact that this patients often experienced conflicts between sexual drives and the constraints of reality. Once opposing drives were in conflict they seemed not to be openly expresses; nevertheless, Freud saw the drives as remaining in force, although blocked and out of awareness. Furthermore, the form that conflicts took within an individual changed as the person developed from childhood into adulthood. During development these conflicts became entirely internalised. Thus, the conflicts which Freud's patients experienced were intrapsychic and existed totally within the individual.

## (4)    Developmental Nature

As Holman (1970) puts it, for every person the "past persists into the present". Thus, a psychoanalytic understanding of any behaviour or symptom requires the tracing of its history. The behaviour or symptom under consideration is understandable only in terms of the behaviour or previous solutions or compromises of an intrapsychic conflict were thought to continue from the past into the present life of the individual. Some motives, aims, or drives may be "frozen" or **fixated** at infantile levels of development and may persist in their relatively undifferentiated form in the adult "life of the individual". Freud believed that an understanding of such fixations is only possible when one looks at human behaviour from a developmental point of view.

## (5)    The Quantitative Aspects of Behaviour

Freud assumed that drives or needs may differ in their intensity or quantity. The variations in the apparent intensity or quantity. The variations in the apparent intensity of suffering among his patients and the marked differences in their concern with themselves or the world around them led Freud to postulate his quantitative aspect of behaviour. For Freud, this was a crucial assumption since he regarded "abnormal" behaviour as only quantitatively different from normal behaviour. Thus, the distinction between what we call abnormal and normal behaviour was a matter of degree, not kind.

## (6)  Behaviour as an Adaptation

Despite the fact that the psychoanalytic perspective is to a very large degree intrapsychic, Freud did not ignore the influence of the external environment on behaviour. Instead, he argued that human behaviour must be understood as response to the demands placed on the person by both the physical and the social environment. This principle has been described by Rapaport and Gill (1967) as the **adaptative point of view**.

These basic principles or assumptions about human behaviour lay the ground work for the psychoanalytic perspective. They comprise Freud's most fundamental ideas about human nature. These themes will recur repeatedly as we examine the psychoanalytic perspective and its unique view of the character and genesis of abnormal behaviour.

## (C)  STAGES OF PSYCHOSEXUAL DEVELOPMENT

The origins of adult fears, hopes, peculiarities, and virtues could be found in the early development of the child, according to the psychoanalytic view. Even before a child can speak or reason, it is engaged in a continual struggle to meet its own biological needs and to gain love and approval from its caretakers. These early struggles of life leave their marks on the character of the person and Freud believed they were of fundamental importance.

Consistent with his basic assumption concerning the importance of psychological development, Freud postulated a series of developmental stages, usually called the **psychosexual stages** of development. The term "sexual" as it is used by Freud has a much broader meaning than the term usually connotes. It refers not only to the stimulation of the genital area but also of other erogenous zones. The principal erogenous zones were thought to be the mouth, the anus and the genital organs.

Freud believed that the erogenous zones were important for the development of personality because they are the first sources of excitation with which the child must contend. In addition, actions that the child undertakes involving the erogenous zones may lead to parental censure. The child must deal with the resulting frustration and anxiety that may occur and these initial modes of coping are of great importance in later development. Thus, the parents' concern with the child's eating, elimination, and genital manipulation are assumed to have great impact on how the child comes to cope with problems later in life.

Freud differentiated three pregenital stages of development. The **Oral stage**, the **Anal stage** and the **Phallic stage**. Following the phallic stage, a period of 5 or 6 years (called the period of latency) occurs, when the dynamics of development are more or less stabilized. Following the latency period comes the final stage of development, the **genital stage**, during adolescence. Table 1-1 sketches the major psychosexual stages and summarizes their most important features.

## Table 1-1: Stages of Psychosexual Activity in the Psychoanalytic Perspective

| | Stages of Psychosexual Development | Erogenous Zone | Prototypical Activity | Later Personality |
|---|---|---|---|---|
| 1. | Oral stage (0 – 2 years) | Mouth | Sucking: incorporation, biting | Oral-incorporative, "sucker", aggressive; oral-sadistic |
| 2. | Anal stage (2 – 3 years) | Anal Sphincter | Urge for elimination strict toilet training rewarded | Anal erotentive or expulsive, productive, creative |
| 3. | Phallic (4 – 5 years) | Genital Organs | Masturbation, autoerotic activity, castration fear, penis envy | Oedipus complex, Electra complex, later relations with men and women |

## THE ORAL STAGE

During the first year of life the predominant erogenous zone is the mouth. Children gratify their hunger through sucking and often incorporate the objects into their mouths for the pleasurable tactile stimulation the objects provide later, as the children develop teeth, biting also becomes an important function in the oral stage. As Munroe (1955) points out, the

Freudian perspective argues that most modes of relating to objects are derived from the oral stage of development.

The two basic modes of oral activity, incorporation and biting, may become "prototypes" for later character traits. Thus, the child who is fixated on an incorporative mode of development may later develop an "oral incorporative" personality. For example, this child may be gullible and therefore "swallow" almost anything he or she is told. On the other hand, if the child is fixated is the biting mode, oral aggression may become the dominant character trait. The child later may become a person who indulges in argumentativeness or verbal hostility. Since the child is almost entirely dependent on the mother for protection and sustenance, the oral stage of development also may have important effects on later adult feelings of dependency.

## THE ANAL STAGE

In the second and third years of development, the child begins to focus on the pressure upon the anal sphincter as a source of discomfort or as a source of erotic pleasure. The natural mode of relieving this discomfort is defecation. However, coincidentally toilet training is initiated by the parents. This usually represents the first instance in which the child must learn to regulate an instinctual impulse, consequently one of the important conflicts between the parents and child occurs.

As toilet training proceeds, the crucial developmental issue is the nature of the relationship between the parents and the child. If the parents are extremely strict and harsh in their methods, the child may held back his faeces and this mode of handling anal elimination becomes a prototype for later behaviour. The child may develop a retentive character in later life, or on the other hand, he or she may, because of frustration and anger at repressive toilet training methods, develop what has been called an "anal expulsive" character organisation, as an extension of having expelled the faeces at inappropriate times during the anal stage. Freud also believed that if the parents praise the child for production of faeces, the child will come to believe that this is an important activity and the product a valuable one. The effect of this mode of parental training in the character of the individual may become the basis for creativity or productivity.

## THE PHALLIC STAGE

During the fourth and fifth years of the child's development, the genital organs become the principal source of satisfaction for the child. The child begins to engage in masturbation and autoerotic activity. The phallic stage is the stage in which the Oedipus complex develops. In general, the Oedipus complex involves the sexual attraction to the parent of the opposite sex and anger or hostility toward the parent of the same sex. Thus, the boy wishes to posses his mother and displace his father and vice versa, in the case of a girl. For Freud, the Oedipus complex was a crucial determinant of later adult attitudes toward the opposite sex and toward people in authority.

In the case of the boy, he imagines that his father is a rival who may harm him for his desire of his mother. Since the genital organs are the major focus of this person, the child associates sensations from his genital organs with his affectionate feeling for his mother. He also fears that his father will remove the offending organs. This Freud described as "castration anxiety". Because of his fear of castration, the boy comes to repress his sexual desire for his mother and to identify with his father.

For the girl, the Oedipus complex has a somewhat different sequence of development. As she discovers that a boy possesses an exterior sexual organ while she possesses non, she holds her mother responsible for her castrated condition. Furthermore, she comes to view her father as a love object because he has the valued organ she wishes to have herself. She also is envious of her father and all other males because they have something she does not have. This envy Freud called "penis envy". The Oedipus complex of the girl does not undergo repression as it did for the boy. Instead, it undergoes some slight modification during this period because of the realistic constraints against sexual relations with her father.

Feminist writers have vigorously criticized psychoanalytic theory on this point. The Oedipus complex both for the boy and the girl during the fourth and fifth years of life were seen by Freud as major landmarks in the development of the child. Furthermore, as we have suggested, the resolution of the Oedipus complex and the modes of relationship that develop from it produce a variety of important modes of adaptation that persist in the later relationships of both males and females to members of their own and the opposite sex.

## THE GENITAL STAGE

Following the period of latency there is a final active stage of psychosexual development in the child. This usually occurs during adolescence from the age of fourteen upwards when the narcissistic or self-oriented concerns of the pregenital stages are replaced to a large degree by realistic object choices in the real world. During the genital stage the child is transformed from a narcissistic self-oriented child into a socialized adult. The child becomes concerned with vocational choice, socialization and peer relationships.

It should be noted, however, that the effects of the pre-genital stages of development do not entirely disappear but remain "fused" with the later effects of the genital stage. According to psychoanalytic theory then, children praised for their "productions" on the toilet may transform this "productive" character trait into a more adult form and become perhaps writers or painters as adults. The final personality organization of the individual is not a product of the genital stage alone but of the residue of each of the stages of development as they persist in the adult character of the individual.

## (D) PSYCHOLOGICAL STRUCTURE

The psychoanalytic perspective that Freud developed delineated three major provinces of the mind. For Freud, these three provinces were the major functional units of mental life. He called these units the **id**, the **ego**, and the **superego** and became the basic building blocks on which his theory of the dynamics of behaviour were based. Table 1-3 summarizes the structural characteristics, functioning principles, and modes of operation of the id, ego and superego.

### The Id

The id is the most primitive province of the personality structure. It contains the instincts (or, more accurately, drive) and is the source of human psychic energy. The function of the id is to discharge energy released in the organism either by internal or external stimulation and to keep the level of tension in the organism as low as possible. Thus, the id seeks to gratify instinctual drives immediately and is said to operate according to the **pleasure principle**.

**Table 1-3: Personality Structure According to the Psychoanalytic Perspective**

| Structure | Functioning Principle | Mode of Operation |
|---|---|---|
| **Id** The instincts, source of psychic energy, biological substratum of personality. | **Pleasure principle** Seeks to gratify instinctual drives immediately. | **Primary process** Direct motor discharge of energy or drive e.g. dreams, wish fulfilment. |
| **Ego** Developed from the id: reality-oriented, judging, executive. | **Reality principle** "Executive function", i.e. moderates demands of instinctual impulses and demands of external reality. | **Secondary process** Differentiates objective from subjective reality; relies on past experience; judges |
| **Superego** Developed from the ego, represents introjection of parental moral standards and values. | **Moral evaluation** Judges right and wrong, "good" and "bad". | **Conscience** Source of moral judgement. Ego ideal image of person child would like to become. |

*Source:* Richard H. Price (1978, p. 4)

The id is the psychological representation of the biological substratum of human personality. It does not develop over time but remains unchanged and unaltered by external reality. For Freud the id is unorganised, "a caos, a cauldron of seething excitement" (Freud, 1933, pp. 103-104).

The id may seek gratification and the discharge of tension directly through a motor reflex or through the primary process, which operates in the following way. If immediate gratification of a wish or drive is impossible, then the memory traces of the individual are activated and an image of the desired object may be produced to gratify the need for tension reduction. This is known as **wish fulfilment**. It is important to realize that the id does not distinguish between the image of the object and the object itself. It makes no distinction between objective reality and subjective reality. Thus, the primary process may produce hallucinations or dreams in order to gratify id instincts or drives. For example, the hungry sleeper may dream of food. The image of the food then serves as the object of tension reduction for the id.

In order to survive in the harsh realities of man's external environment, however, the id will not suffice. Thus, a second structure of mind develops from the id, and the basic function of this structure is to deal with external reality.

## The Ego

As the constraints of the external world impinge upon the organism, a part of the id develops and becomes more differentiated. This new structure is called the ego. The role of the ego is to pursue gratification but at the same time to take account of the demands of external reality. Thus, the ego is said to be operated according to the **reality principle**.

The ego acts as a mediator between id impulses and reality. However, as Freud points out, it does not actually displace id impulses but acts to assure the gratification of these impulses. For example, the ego may function to delay a short-term gratification only to assure a more enduring form of gratification that may occur at a later time.

The mode of operation by which this "executive function" is carried out is called the **secondary process**. The secondary process differentiates between subjective and objective reality. The secondary process relies on past experience and the evaluation of this experience to make judgements about the most appropriate means of obtaining gratification. In order to carry out this task the ego must be a highly organised and differentiated structure. It is a structure in contact with both the conscious perceptions of the external world and the incessant demands of the id. The psychological functions of action, thought, memory, and perception are all used by the ego in order to evaluate the experience and to provide realistic gratification. Freud (1940, 1949) described the function of the ego in the following:

> Its constructive function (of the ego) consists in interposing the demand made by instinct and the action that satisfies it, an intellective activity which, after considering the present state of things and weighing up earlier experiences, endeavours by means of experimental actions to calculate consequences of the proposed line of conduct. In this way ego comes to a decision whether the attempt to obtain satisfaction is to be carried out or postponed or whether it may not be necessary for the demand of the instinct to be altogether suppressed as being dangerous (p. 110).

Thus we see that the ego functions to maintain the organism in the face of "three harsh hasters", (a) the id's demands of total fulfilment of biological impulses, (b) the persistent demands of external reality, and (c) the injunctions of the superego.

## The Superego

Freud also wished to have a way of representing the domain of moral values in human behaviour. For this purpose he postulated the superego as an additional portion of the personality structure.

The superego develops from a portion of the ego. As children grow they are influenced by their parents through reward and punishment. In this way they learn values from their parents, and as the children identify themselves with their parents, they internalise or **introject** these values.

Thus a portion of the ego, the superego, comes to evaluate acts according to moral standards and the children learn to judge themselves using these standards. They come to react with shame or pride when evaluating their own actions.

The superego is usually identified with the idea of **conscience**. In addition, however, a second system is associated with the superego, that of the **ego ideal**. The ego ideal is a composite of the values the children have learned. The ego ideal becomes important for growing children as an image of the sort of person they should strive to become. Usually parents are the sources of this ego ideal in children and become the person with whom they identify. But later, particularly in adolescence, children may come to identify with other figures as the ego ideal.

Both the ego ideal and the conscience aspects of the superego play a crucial role in the socialization of children. The dictates and values of society are transmitted through the parents to the children, and the parents become the first representations of the society with which children must ultimately cope.

We can see that these three structures represent potentially conflicting motives and goals for the individual. Although the ego may attempt to mediate these conflicts, situations in the life of the individual will continually arise in which conflict is inevitable.

## (E)    ANXIETY AND DEFENSES AGAINST IT

Freud believed that the conflict between the id impulses – primarily sexual and aggressive instincts – and the restraining influences of the ego and the superego – constituted the motivating source of such behaviour. Because society condemns free expression of aggression and sexual behaviour, such impulses cannot be immediately and directly expressed. Children learn early that they may not handle their genitals in public or hit their siblings. They eventually internalise parental restrictions on impulse satisfaction, thus forming the superego. The more restraints a society (or its representatives, the parents) places on impulse expression, the greater the potential for conflict between the three parts of the personality.

The desires of the id are powerful forces that must be expressed in some way; prohibiting their expression does not abolish them. Individuals with an urge to do something for which they will be punished become anxious. One way of reducing anxiety is to express the impulse in disguised form, thereby avoiding punishment by society and condemnation by the superego. Aggressive impulses, for example, may be displaced to racing sports cars or to championing political causes.

Another method of reducing anxiety, called **repression**, is to push the impulse out of awareness into the unconscious. Those methods of anxiety reduction, called **defense mechanisms**, are means of defending oneself against painful anxiety. They are never totally successful in relieving tension, and the residue may spill over in the form of nervousness or restlessness, which as Freud pointed out, is the price we must pay for being civilized. Presumably, a society that placed no restrictions on free expression of the id's instincts would produce people completely free of anxiety or tension. But such a society would probably not survive for long; all societies must place some restrictions on behaviour for the well-being of the group.

Defense mechanisms form the basis of Freud's theory of neurotic and psychotic behaviour. At this point, we will note only that people differ in the balance among id, ego, and superego systems and in the defenses they use against anxiety. The individual's approach to a problem situation reflects his or her manner of coping with the conflicting demands of the id, ego, and superego.

**Notes:**

1. This chapter benefited from Richard H. Price, **Abnormal Behaviour: Perspectives in Conflict.** Second Edition. (New York: Holt, Rinehart and Winston, 1978, chapter two.

# CHAPTER FOUR

## MAN'S SOCIAL NATURE

### SECTION (A)

**INTRODUCTION**

The major objective of this chapter is to show the nature of the distinctive social psychological perspective or viewpoint about exactly <u>how</u> and <u>why</u> societies, communities, social groups, and social aggregates - in short, <u>the totality of the social milieu</u> - which envelopes or encapsulates individual human beings, and within which all individuals live all of their lives from birth through death, exert some noteworthy influences upon the lives of individuals, if at all they actually do so.

It is worthwhile to point out that there had existed both the purely sociological as well as the purely psychological perspectives about the nature of human behaviour before the advent of the social psychological-perspective in order for the reader to be able to more properly follow all what I will say about the distinctive nature of the social psychological viewpoint about the complex relationships between societies and individuals in this chapter.

For, social psychology actually begins its own analysis of human behaviour from the fundamental premise or assumption that both psychology and sociology give some essentially valid and useful but too much one-sided accounts about the nature of human beings and human behaviour. And that as a result, each of them by itself alone does not, and cannot, give a full, comprehensive, and adequate account about human behaviour.

Social psychology attempts to fuse, combine or synthesize some of the most central and relevant elements from both sociology and psychology together, and comes up with what amounts to a "coin metaphor" viewpoint about the complex nature of human beings or human behaviour. This distinctively social psychological "coin metaphor" perspective simply states that both the individual and society are inseparable, very much necessary and complementary to each other, and that as such they represent the two sides of the same "coin", which may be called either "man's social-nature", or that "man is a social animal". On the basis of this coin metaphor viewpoint, social psychology makes its most general and fundamental contention about human behaviour to the effect that the predominant nature of the behavioural characteristics and predilections (e.g., the human personality, motivations, perception, cognition or knowledge, beliefs, cultural norms and values, roles, skills, statuses etc) of individual human beings are largely a function of as well as a reflection of the predominant dynamic processes of the social structure and culture of the particular society in which they happen to live at any particular point in time, ceteris paribus.

This is the most central and important hypothesis which underlies much of what social psychologists study about all of the several different forms of human behaviours. It must be very carefully noted that like any other hypothetical statement in any scientific discipline, the above statement should not also be regarded as being a kind of gospel truth. Because, in actuality, it does not at all represent an already completely proven or dogmatic statement of fact as such. But rather, this hypothesis merely represents a kind of heuristic device, that is, a kind of an initial and basic working assumption about how the generality of individual human beings appear to be connected with society. AS an assumption, this hypothesis (like any other hypothesis in any science) is intended to guide any social psychologist when he is conducting an empirical research, by telling him that this or that is <u>how individuals "appear" to be influenced by their society, or vice-versa</u>. But in the final analysis, it is exactly what the social psychology researcher himself actually finds out that should, ideally, determine what he should write about the specific nature of the human behaviour which he himself observed. Thus, for example, if a social psychology researcher finds that the pattern of individual behaviour which he has observed tallies with what this hypothesis postulates, then he will tend to conclude that the hypothesis has actually guided him properly, and that its prediction about how individual behaviours are really influenced by society is true or correct to a great extent. But, in contrast, if what the social psychology researcher has observed empirically differs a great deal from what this hypothesis predicts, then he will likely conclude that the hypothesis may be modified, clarified, or improved upon. **In short, with the aid of the above-mentioned hypothesis, social psychologists constantly seek to find out empirically the exact extent to which societies actually exert significant influences on the behaviours of various individuals, if at all they really do so.**

# SECTION (B)
# MAN AS A SOCIAL ANIMAL

Exactly what should be understood by the student of social psychology by the statement that "man is a social animal"? There is probably no clear - cut or self-evident "meaning" of that statement which the student of social psychology can easily lay his/her hand upon as such. But instead, by virtue of the fact that this social psychological view about man's nature was distilled from both the sociological and psychological views about man's nature, it might be more worthwhile for us to very quickly examine both the sociological and psychological viewpoints, in order for us, hopefully, to understand the social psychological synthetic or eclectic viewpoint that "man is a social animal", in its proper perspective.

## The Sociological Viewpoint About Man's Nature

The sociological view about man's nature may be briefly summarized as follows: That no individual human being really has any separate or distinctive identity of his or her own as such. But that rather, every individual human being is an integral part and parcel of the **social groups** and societies to which he/she belongs, and in terms of whose laws, norms, values and the like he/she lives his/her life from birth through death. In short, sociologists assert and strongly emphasize that man is completely a product of his society, and that as such his nature is predominantly "social", that is, a replica of the "social nature" of his/her society.

For example, Aristotle, one of the ancient Greek philosophers, observed a very long, long time ago that "man is a social animal". Later, from the equally famous words of John Donne (the 17th century English poet and theologian) we also learn that:

*"No man is an island, entire of itself, Everyman is a piece of the continent, a part of the main."*

Modern proponents of the sociological view that "man is a social being" include Auguste Comte, Emile Durkheim, Charles Horton Cooley, etc.

## The Psychological Viewpoint about Man's Nature

On the other hand, the proponents of the psychological viewpoint about man's nature also appear to be fully aware that individuals are really parts and parcels of some social groups/societies. But then they strongly argue that although societies constantly seek to mould or even constrain the interests and behaviours of individuals, that individuals themselves make genuine, arduous, sustained, and sometimes quite successful efforts to resist and prevent society from determining their behaviours to a great extent. Psychologists say that they are more interested in studying/analyzing these various ways and manners which several individuals make to extricate themselves from the clutches of their social groups, communities and societies, in order for them to be able to largely determine their own individual behaviours by themselves. Some interesting examples of how individuals attempt to accomplish these individualistic existentialist objectives are as follows:

(1)     The constant struggle by some individuals to gain more and more "personal freedom" from their parents, teachers, bosses, spouses, friends, Government, etc.

(2)     The various efforts which many individuals make to rely, trust, believe, or repose confidence in only themselves in many of the things which they do in their everyday lives.

(3)     The various subtle or otherwise crudely overt acts of selfishness, self-centredness, or self-interest which are perpetrated by various individuals.

(4)     The various efforts which some individuals make to be opportunistic, that is, to exploit some strategic and auspicious circumstances to gain some credits for themselves, usually (but not necessarily) at the expense of other people or the social situation, itself.

These and several of other similar things which many individuals actually do day in and day out around all of us in our different walk's of life, can really be referred to as being predominantly "individualistic" forms of human behaviour. A sample of some of the interesting views by some of the major proponents who advocate or emphasize these "individualistic" aspects of man's complex nature is, as follows:-

John Stuart Mill, the classic 19th century English individualist says that:

"Men are not, when brought together, converted into another kind of substance."

While the 19th century American poet, Walt Whitman (1819-1892) asks:

"What do you suppose will satisfy the (human) soul, except to walk free and own no superior?"

Max Stirner answers, in effect, that:

"It is not recognized in the full amplitude of the world that all freedom is essentially self-liberation - that I can have only so much freedom as I procure for myself by my owness."

According to the 18th/19th century precocious and versatile German scholar Johann Welfgang von Goethe (1749-1832):

"As soon as you trust yourself, you will know how to live."

The similarly encyclopedic and very prolific 19th century English social philosopher, Herbert Spencer (1820-1903) also contends that:

"Volumes might be written upon the impiety of the (so-called) pious (people, who claim to be the custodians as well as the arbiters of their respective society's moral and ethical culture)."

The contemporary American novelist Irving Wallace adds, in effect, that:

"Poke (i.e., probe) any (such so-called pious person or) saint enough, and you (will) touch (upon) self-interest (in him or her)."

From a slightly different individualistic point of view, Rudyard Kipling (1865-1936), the highly famed Englishman who won the very highly converted Nobel Prize for Literature in 1907 gives the following piece of advice to any potentially ambitious" or self-centred person:

"He travels the fastest who travels alone."

Similarly, according to the American writer, David Seabury:

"Don't worry about the whole world: if you do it will overwhelm you. Worry about one wave at a time. Please (only) yourself. Do something for yourself, and the rest will fall in line."

But perhaps the most audacious advocacy for individuals to be opportunistic and to constantly exploit any social situation in which they find themselves to the best of their abilities has been made by the world's foremost and perhaps the most sagacious master of literature himself, that is in the person of, William Shakespeare who said that:

"Why, then the world's mine oyster, which I with
sword will open".

Again, talking about the fact that it is sometimes (or always) necessary for individuals to mostly depend or rely on themselves in all or almost all of the things which they seek to do, John Godfrey Saxe has this very important injunction or message to give to interested individuals:

"In battle or business, whatever the game,
In law or in love, it is every the same;
In the struggle for power, or the scramble for pelf,
Let this be your motto,
rely on (only) yourself!"

Shakespeare, again, gives an identical formula to guide an individual's behaviour, as follows:

"This above all: to thine own self be true,
And it must follow, as the night the day,
(That) thou canst not then be false to any men".

I will like to conclude these indisputably interesting and educative views by the proponents of the "psychological" or "individualistic" aspects of human behaviour by quoting what I personally regard as being the more or less most eternally endearing advisory view by one John Greenleaf Whittier, as follows:

"For of all sad words of tongue or pen, The saddest
are these: "It might have been!"

## The Social Psychological Viewpoint About Man's Nature

Well, from the foregoing, we have heard from the so-called horses' mouths themselves - on both the "sociological" and the "psychological" sides of our "coin metaphor". The most important inference which we as social psychology students must make is that the views by both the sociologists and psychologists about man's nature are actually interesting and valid to a great extent, but they are also too much one-sided. That is, their views place an unduly great emphasis on only some aspects of the complex nature of human behaviour, at the expense of other equally important aspects. As a result, neither the sociological nor the psychological viewpoint can actually provide us with a full, comprehensive, or adequate account about the very complex nature of the mutual interrelationship between individuals and their societies. Consequently, we will accept and constantly attempt to test the usefulness of the social psychological attempt to synthesize both the sociological and psychological views under the new rub ric called the "coin metaphor". In other worlds, as social psychologists, we will from henceforth hold **the viewpoint that both society and the individual are inseparable, they are necessary and complementary to each others, and that they are the two major sides which make up the "coin" (that is, "the individual human being"), otherwise called "the social animal".**

I think that at this juncture it is now auspicious to answer the question which I posed at the very beginning of this sub-section of this chapter. At the risk of belabouring it, the question again is: Exactly what should be understood by the student of social psychology by the statement that "Man is a "social animal"? The answer is as follows: According to social psychology, in any and every given social action situation, one will really find that there is always a very subtle but obvious kind of a dialectical admixture of both relatively distinctive "social" as well as

115

relatively distinctive "psychological/ individualistic" human behavioural elements/factors/forces/ influences/ tendencies/motives/ interests/problems/results; and that neither of them can be honestly ignored, over-looked, or subsumed under the other. That although it is really true that social groups/societies make strenuous efforts to mould/domesticate/ transform individuals into their "social" images, they never actually succeed in doing so completely - for, in the final analysis, virtually every individual human being still retains some peculiar/ distinctive/idiosyncratic behavioural traits, which is why every individual has his/her own relatively distinctive or unique personality. For example, it is really true that in real life, no two individual human beings - no matter how similar they may be - they never actually have an exactly identical "personality" or "behaviour", not even "identical twins". In short, although every and all human being(s) really learn(s) and acquire(s) a lot of "social" behavioural characteristics and tendencies (e.g. language, skills, aspirations, roles, attitudes, values, etc) from the various social groups and societies in which they may find themselves" from time to time, they do not therefore become automatically or completely converted into "social entitles". That is because to the extent that every human being still possesses and continually acts out his/her own basic "individual biological" instincts, impulses, reflexes, and the like, to that extent social psychology strongly argues that every man/woman still perpetually remains an "animal" (That is, a "biological organism"), to great extent.

Similarly, on the other hand, that although it is also really true that virtually all or almost all individual human beings make deliberate, strenuous, sustained and conscious or unconscious efforts to assert their individuality/freedom/ independence, or to exploit and take undue advantages of other fellow human beings as well as social situations, they never actually succeed in doing so completely. "In the final analysis they also make some significant "sacrifices" or "payments" in exchange for whatever they got from other people, and most importantly, they still perpetually remain mutually interdependent, upon and they also remain as integral parts and parcels of the various social groups and societies, within whose "social" contexts they interact amongst themselves and achieve all of their numerous, varied and diverse existential objectives (e.g. food, shelter, education, employment, reproduction, defense, emotional gratifications, etc). To that extent, therefore, social psychology also strongly argues that every man/woman eventually becomes a "social" phenomenon to a great extent.

In sum, we can really see from the foregoing analysis that both the "social" and the "psychological" (or "animal or biological") human behavioural elements appear to always co-exist as separate/independent phenomena in every individual human being. That is why social psychology states that they represent the two major relatively distinctive "sides" or "sets" of elements which make up the totality of each individual's behavioural characteristics and predilections. Consequently, unlike sociology which over-emphasizes the primacy of the "social" elements in human behaviour; and psychology which over-emphasizes the primacy of the "psychological/ individualistic" elements in human behaviour; social-psychology, as a kind of an amalgam of the above two disciplines, simultaneously recognizes, and equally emphasizes the primacies of both the "social" as well as the "psychological/individualistic" elements in any and every form of human behaviour, and/or in any and every type of social action situation, at any particular point in time, and in any particular place across the whole world, all other things being well. So, the above account concisely shows exactly what social psychology means by its statement that "man is a social animal".

I am strongly convinced that from all what I have said above, I have sufficiently and clearly explained the above-mentioned fundamental theoretical orientation of social psychology. As a result I also expect that every person who is reading this chapter should from henceforth be able to <u>easily</u> and <u>accurately</u> accomplish the following <u>two major analytical tasks:</u>

(1)  Distinguish between the sociological, psychological, and social-psychological viewpoints about man's nature, or the nature of human behaviour.

(2)  Pin-point, identify, and concisely state what is meant

    (a)      the "coin metaphor"; and/or

    (b)      the statement that "man is a social animal" - in social psychology.

# SECTION (C)
# MAN'S SOCIAL NATURE

The individual human being is a social animal, to a great extent. In other words, human beings are basically gregarious. That is, they need and constantly seek the company and assistance of one another, no matter how individualistic, free, or independent that they may also aspire to and/or claim to be, as well. Individuals do virtually little or nothing by themselves alone and/or in complete isolation from other individuals.

The "idea" as to whether an individual can live all alone by himself/herself is symptomatic of the so-called Robinson Crusoe syndrome of human existence. But the Robinson Crusoe idea of human existence is a myth, a kind of literary imagination, which does not have any foundation in reality whatsoever. It was Daniel Defoe, the brilliant 18th century English novelist, who probably first created the myth in his novel entitled Robinson Crusoe. In that interesting novel, Defoe tried to imagine, and then sought to examine, the possibility of a man living all alone by himself, and in a contented manner, in an isolated island; but he came up with the conclusion that was both impossible and impracticable. For example, Defoe's fictional character, whom he called Robinson Crusoe, suddenly found himself ship-wrecked in the middle of an enormous ocean, and then later he became marooned on a completely isolated island, which initially had seemed to be devoid of human life. So, after Mr. Robinson regained consciousness, he felt the pangs of hunger, thirst, heat, etc. He then set about to make his first initial efforts to procure, for these as well as his other existential needs/ wants. He erroneously thought that he was living, all alone by himself, and that he was no longer in his erstwhile English society. But it soon became apparent that Mr. Robinson was grossly mistaking. Granted that he was actually then living a kind of solitary life, at least at the initial stage of his supposed sojourn on that desolate island, he was not even then, strictly speaking, living alone, as such. In social psychology, we make a very crucial distinction between living "alone" and living in a "solitary" manner. The former connotes a situation in which an individual lives in a state in which he is, at least, theoretically, supposed to be completely independent, self-sufficient, and completely dispenser with any other fellow human being, for any and all of his existential needs/wants (e.g. food, shelter, ideas, knowledge, 'beliefs, values, etc). Whereas the latter (i.e., living in a "solitary" manner) means mostly "physical isolation". That is, that although at some given period of time an individual may be living separately by only himself/ herself in a particular place, he/she continues to be dependent upon other fellow human beings for his/her basic existential needs/wants during that particular period of time in which he/she, is living in voluntary or forced "solitary" confinement.

Thus, Mr. Robinson never ever lived alone, even on that island, because he was still behaving as the Englishman from York (that he was before he found himself on that island). For example, he still invoked the Holy Bible and prayed to his tribal - English God(s). Furthermore, Robinson Crusoe later found another man, called Friday, on the same island, and they soon began the building of another society. Consequently, as we now better know, Daniel Defoe's idea of a Robinson Gusoe man living all alone by himself and in a completely independent and self-sufficient manner could not even materialize. As a result, it has remained ever since from then up to date a mere fictional creation, that is, a merely literary imagination, and as such it amounts to a kind of myth, which is not isomorphic with reality at all.

The other relevant myth which is also frequently used for illustrative purposes in the Social and Human Behavioural

# SOCIAL PSYCHOLOGY

Sciences was the one which was conducted by the celebrated 19th century Russian novelist called Dostoyevsky. In his stories about <u>Devils</u> one man whom he called Kirilov commits suicide, ostensibly to demonstrate his "perfect freedom". In a way, suicide, that is, the act of killing one's self, should have been the only really completely individualistic act which is open to the individual human being. But, unfortunately, since the very distinguished French Sociologist Emile Durkheim carried out his classic study of that human act, as published in his book entitled <u>Suicide</u> (1897), it is also even no longer possible to make it an exception to the general rule. For example, Durkheim identified (1) altruism, (2) egoism, (3) anomie, and (4) fatalism, as representing both the four major types of suicide as well as the four major grounds upon which individuals would want to commit suicide, and reached the conclusion that suicide on any of these four grounds is by no means minimally independent of social influences or conditions.

Thus, the human act of every individual human being involves, in one way or another, his/her membership of some social group/society, including, the supposedly most "personal" act of killing one's self. By the statement that humans are **social** or **gregarious** is therefore meant that they take some due cognizance of, and/or act in some concert, with one another in their everyday lives. In other words, all individual human beings must take some cognizance of, and/or actually engage in some concerted actions with other follow individual human beings, in order for them to be able to pursue and achieve (or fail to achieve) all of their various different existential wants and needs (e.g., getting food, shelter, education, entertainment, religious salvation, peace of mind, etc). And all of the social ways as well as the social contexts in which people accomplish all of their existential wants/needs make up man's social nature.

121

The term "man's social nature" simply refers to the fact that individual human beings do not ever have any completely independent existence of their own as such. But rather, all of us individual human beings are born into and live the whole of our various life spans from birth to death as members of some society, which exerts a very profound and pervasive influence over every aspect and stage of our lives. As soon as we are born, our society gets to work on us and transforms us to a very great extent from merely biological into social/ biological organisms (which is more conveniently called "human 'beings"). For example, the language which one speaks is not an individual's biological inheritance, but rather it is a social acquisition from the social groups/communities in which one grows up. Both language and environment help to determine the character of one's thoughts, ideas, attitudes, values and beliefs. Therefore, all of the various social ways as well as all of the various social agencies or contexts (e.g, families, schools, organizations, gangs, communities, etc) by which society moulds and determines the behavioural characteristics and lives of individuals, or in which individuals themselves inexorably depend upon society, constitute what social psychology calls "man's social nature".

Consequently, to go back to what Aristotle said, "man is really a social animal", to a great extent. In fact, "what this really means is that man's nature is much more overwhelmingly/ predominantly social, than animalistic, biological, or individualistic. To properly grasp this basic thesis, is the foremost task before all students of social psychology, Man is not unless he is social; whatever he is .depends on his social being, and whatever he makes of his social being is irrevocably bound to what he makes of himself. He has the ability to master his internal being (e.g, his own unique biological make-ups, such as talents, beauties, emotions, instincts impulses, etc); but the main way to accomplish self-mastery leads to his joining with others like himself in various social acts. Potentially, every man is free to choose; social laws, unlike those of nature, can be flaunted and, above all, rewritten. In fact, however, social laws penetrate individual existence so deeply that most escapes are limited in scope and often lead from compliance with one set of laws to even fuller compliance with another set of social laws. The confines of social life are frequently composed of other people in the same predicament; hence, in principle, the transformation of social life can be propelled by give-and-take among the fellow individual members themselves. While individualistic action is very possible - and also quite necessary in some occasions or circumstances – it cannot also itself be properly understood-unless against the background of the social ways and social contexts of which it is a part, on which it builds, or against which it reacts.

# SECTION (D)
# THE ORGANIZATION OF MAN'S SOCIAL NATURE

The social self, however, is not a random combination of persons; but rather it is relatively structured and its various movements and actions are relatively organized in various degrees. Individuals actively participate in their social environment, they act and interact, some even lead others, but the only context of human existence is some form of relatively organized social grouping.

Whether his particular topic/subject of study is how and why certain individuals acquire and act out their own predominantly tribal/traditional cultural ways of life; or how and why certain other individuals acquire and act out certain alien values (e.g., Western values); or the increasing incidence of psychopathic persons in a community; or the pattern of individual behaviour in a children's neighbourhood friendship clique; or the role of women in an underground criminal gang; or how to be a Nigerian; or whatever else; the student of social psychology gives the predominant proportion of his attention to discovering how individuals and groups relate to one another. His task is to identify the pattern of personal and group relations which influence individual conduct and social institutions. In social psychology the term "social organization" is used to refer to any and all of the patterns of individual and group relations/interactions with one another.

Thus, when used in its broadest sense, the term "social organization" is coterminous with "social fabric", "social life" and "social order". All these terms simply suggest that human behaviours and relations are closely interwoven and that strains on one part may weaken the whole fabric in unanticipated ways. These terms also emphasize that there exists a significant amount of harmony, orderliness, predictability, interdependence, and cohesiveness, in human co-existence. Social organization also consists of all the tendencies, forces, and relations/interactions which isolate individuals and groups and which foster disharmony, disunity, individualism, and conflict. For example, the social organization/social fabric/social order/social life of any higher educational institution, such as a University, may categorize non-academic staff from academic staff and thereby create conflicts of interest among these and other various social categories within the enterprise/establishment.

By itself the world organization connotes a technical arrangement of parts and does not suggest the complexity, texture, and dynamics of human association. The adjective social before organization emphasizes that individual and group relations are mostly adaptive outcomes of social processes.

Social organization emerges out of day-to-day interaction, out of problem-solving, conflict, co-operation, and accommodation.

A good way to grasp the general idea of social organization/social fabric/social order/social life is to examine any familiar case, for example, a village, a town, a city, a political party, a polytechnic, an extended family group, etc. Let us examine the case of a town, say, Benin City. In Benin City, there is a wide variety of individuals and social groups, some permanent and formally recognized, others formed ad hoc for special tasks and occasions. In addition, but less discernible, are .the lines/channels of communication and influence best known only to the most active inhabitant in the city (including indigenous Benins as well as all non-Benins). The Oredo local government may be a "sandbox" with little power and little communication" with the inhabitants as a whole; or it may be a source of effective leadership. None of this can be read from an official description of the city's authority structure. The social organization of Benin City can be discovered only in the course of practical living experience or through systematic inquiry. It is a dynamic, living thing, changing from time to time.

## Social Systems
In pursuing the study of social organization/social fabric/social order/social life, and whatever else that contributes towards the constitution of man's social nature, the social psychologist often uses the concept of <u>social system.</u> In its most basic and relevant sense, the concept of "social system" simply means that any, every, and all social phenomena (including individual human beings and social groups, and all of the various ways and manners in which they act and interact with one another) are inter d open dent upon one another. With the use of the concept of social system, any relatively distinctive/separate social phenomena, facts, units, (e.g. any of the various things which individuals and social groups say and/or do) are studied/analyzed as parts of larger, interconnected wholes.

The concept of social system is useful for two reasons. First, it encourages a <u>contextual</u> view of individual and group behaviour. For example, by studying the social system of a family group or a neighbourhood, it is possible to observe the limits that constrain participants as well as the opportunities opened up to them. Decisions and activities are seen in context, that is, as conditioned by the social situation.

Second, the idea of social system invites attention to **relationships** that are not ordinarily visible and for which there are no commonsense names. For example, the interdependence of medical practitioners and patients constitutes a social system.

Social systems may be small or large, stable or unstable, harmonious or stressful. The idea of systems analysis of human social behaviours largely encourages the analyst to look for the **contexts** in which the behaviours occur and the **connections** between the various actors and/or actresses.

## Levels of Social Organization

There are literally thousands of diverse and varied forms or types of social organizations and social systems within and by means of which all of us human beings establish contact with, act towards, respond to, interact with, and exert certain positive and/or negative influences upon one another as we seek to pursue and hope to achieve any one of our virtually uncountable diverse and varied types of existential needs and wants in our every day lives in every human society across the whole world. However, all of them may, for analytical convenience, be classified into three, broad categories, namely,

(1)     the interpersonal level,

(2)     the Group level, and

(3)     the social order level, as shown in Figure 2/1:

Each of these three categories consists of several different specific types of social organizations and social systems.

## Figure 2/1: Levels of Social Organization

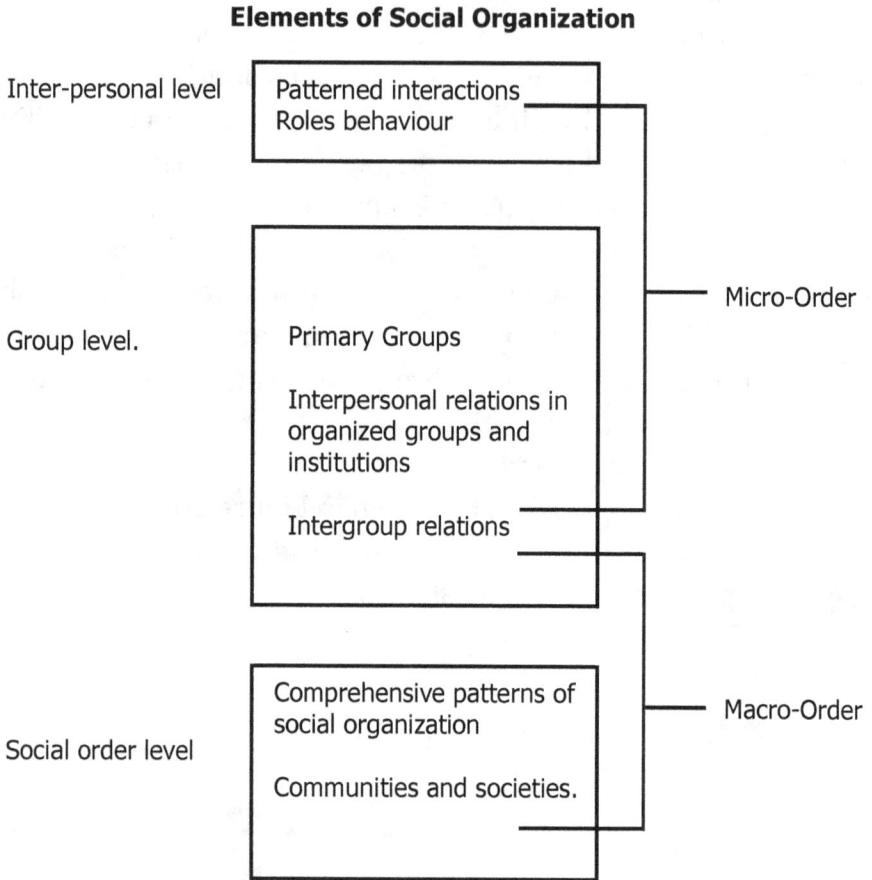

**Elements of Social Organization**

| | | |
|---|---|---|
| Inter-personal level | Patterned interactions<br>Roles behaviour | |
| Group level. | Primary Groups<br><br>Interpersonal relations in organized groups and institutions<br><br>Intergroup relations | Micro-Order |
| Social order level | Comprehensive patterns of social organization<br><br>Communities and societies. | Macro-Order |

*Source:* Adapted from **Sociology: A Text With Adapted Readings** by L. Broom and P. Selzuick (1973, page 21), Harper and Brow, New York, U.S.A.

## SECTION (E)
## SUMMARY AND CONCLUSION

From the standpoint of social psychology, all of us individual human beings are social animals or social beings to a great extent. As biological organisms (of the Mammalian Species), we possess certain basic and irrevocable biological behavioural traits e.g. instincts, impulses, emotions, drives, feelings, lenses, reflexes, energies, talents, etc. By themselves alone they maybe wayward, wild dangerous, etc. But either by chance or by some design, we human beings are also born "social", that is, we are born into the midst of our fellow human beings wherein we live and from which we acquire certain indispensable social behavioural traits, e.g. language, disciplines, skills, roles, etc.

This social midst or context, which is comprised by fellow human beings, is not haphazard, but rather it is relatively structured or organized and it is generally called social environment/social organization/social fabric/social life/social order. It is further subdivided into several sizes, which range from the smallest unit of social organization/social fabric/social order/social life called "interpersonal relations", through the medium size ones called "social groups", to the most comprehensive/inclusive size, called "societies". All individual human beings are all born into and belong to all of these various forms of social organizations at the same time. They jointly help to mould and transform the raw and natural biological behavioural traits of the individual into their own social behavioural images, to a great extent. In this respect, every individual learns, acquires and subsequently acts out within his various social environments, the language, ideas, norms, values, skills, roles, disciplines, habits, and any other socially acceptable ways of acting towards, relating to, and interacting with others which every individual must acquire and utilize before he/she can obtain all of his/her basic existential needs/wants. All of the social organizations and all of the "social" ways of behaviour which they impart to the individual constitute "man's social nature".

AS a social science, social psychology is only qualified to study these various social aspects of human beings. Thus, although social psychology recognizes the persistence of man's biological or animalistic nature in man's everyday behaviours, since it is not a natural science (such as biology, anatomy, physiology, biochemistry, etc) it is not, therefore, qualified to scientifically study and make major pronouncements about the exact role which is played by these purely animalistic tendencies of human beings in their overall behaviours. But rather, as a social science, social psychology is qualified to scientifically study/analyze and make major pronouncements about the exact role which is played by the purely social contexts, social organizations and social ways of behaviour which also constitute integral parts of the overall behaviours of most human beings. As a result, social psychology focuses more on **man's social nature**, and leaves off **man's biological nature** to biologists, psychiatrists, geneticists, physiologists, anatomists, biochemists, microbiologists, etc, who are specifically trained and qualified to study and analyze them in greater or details. However, unlike sociology, which also specializes in studying/ analyzing man's social nature, social psychology is the only social science which specializes in studying/analyzing man's social nature vis-a-vis the various individual human beings themselves. In other words, social psychology does not study/analyze patterns of social interactions, social groups, communities and societies as ends in themselves, but rather it studies/analyzes them largely as the means or backgrounds in terms of which both individual/groups behaviours occur, and as such in terms of which individual and group behaviours themselves can be best understood.

# CHAPTER FIVE

# MOTIVATION

## INTRODUCTION

Managers need to be concerned about the levels of behaviours and performance of the various individuals and groups they work with. Managers in all the different types of organizations are continually faced with the fact that vast differences exist in the performance of various individuals involved in handling tasks. Some workers always perform at high levels, they need little or no direction, and appear to enjoy what they are doing. On the other hand, other people perform only at marginal levels, they require constant attention, and are often absent from their work stations.

The reasons for these differences in the behaviours and performances of individuals are many, varied, and complex. On the one hand we could attribute some of these differences to certain individual characteristics, such as personality, intelligence, or ability.

On the other hand, we could also focus on organizational influences such as the job, the supervisors' style, or the reward system used by the organization as contributing to these differences in behaviour and performance. The core concept associated with each of these properties is **motivation**.

Our discussion of motivation in this chapter is divided into two major sections as follows:- First, an attempt will be made to define motivation and to stress its importance to social work managers in organizations. And second, we will present a review of some of the many motivational theories that have been developed, including both the early managerial and psychological approaches and the current contemporary theories. We will also provide a selected review of the many research studies on each theory.

## Definition of Motivation:

The term **motivation** originates from the Latin word movere, which means "to move." However, from the past many years to date of the frequent uses and applications of this concept in many diverse contexts, the term has acquired a more expanded and complex meaning than its original simple literal meaning. For example, motivation theorists have developed many different viewpoints about motivation that place emphasis on different aspects of the concept. On the whole, the differing views about motivation have led so far to the placing of emphasis on three major different aspects of motivation, as follows:

1. The analysis of motivation that concentrates on factors that **arouse** or **incite** a person's activities.
2. Motivation is process-oriented, and concerns choice, direction, and goals.
3. Motivation also concerns how behaviour is **started, sustained,** or **stopped** and what kind of subjective reaction is present in the person while this is going on.

These three different areas of emphasis will serve as the basis for our discussion of the contemporary theories of motivation in this lecture.

## Exhibit 5-1: A Basic Motivation Model

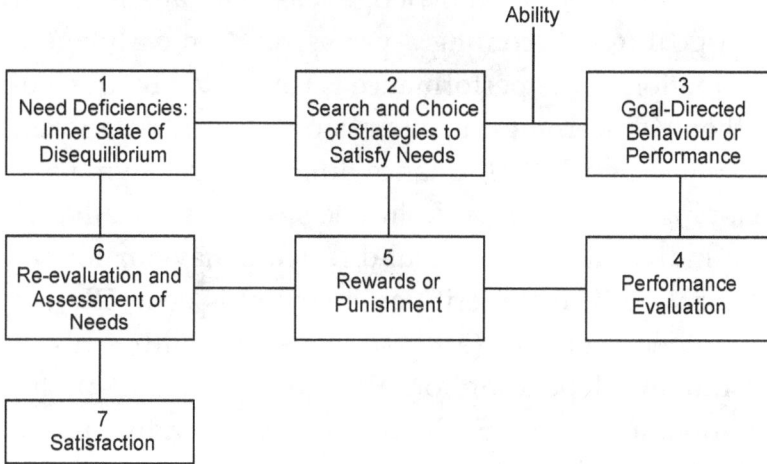

Ability

| 1 Need Deficiencies: Inner State of Disequilibrium | 2 Search and Choice of Strategies to Satisfy Needs | 3 Goal-Directed Behaviour or Performance |
|---|---|---|
| 6 Re-evaluation and Assessment of Needs | 5 Rewards or Punishment | 4 Performance Evaluation |

7 Satisfaction

## A Basic Motivational Model

Building upon the above-mentioned three major areas of emphasis in contemporary motivational studies, we can now provide a basic model of motivation that incorporates the key concepts of needs, drives, goals, and rewards. The initial step in developing the basic motivation model is to relate these variables in a sequential or process framework, as shown in exhibit 4-1, which will provide a foundation for our discussion of the different motivational approaches in this lecture.

The model presents motivation as a multi-step process. First, the arousal of a **need** creates a state of disequilibrium (i.e. tension) within the individual that he or she will try to reduce through his or her behaviour (i.e doing something about the arousal). Second, the individual will **search** for and **choose** strategies to satisfy these needs. Third, the individual will engage in **goal-directed behaviour** or performance to carry out the selected strategy. An important individual characteristic, ability, is seen as intervening between the choice of behaviour and the actual behaviour. This is to recognise that individuals may or may not have the necessary background (i.e., ability, skills, experience, or knowledge base) to attain a particular chosen goal (e.g. becoming a professor at an early age. Fourth, an evaluation of the performance is conducted by the individual (or others) concerning the success of his or her performance in achieving the goal. Performance directed at satisfying a need for developing a sense of pride in one's work is usually evaluated by the individual. While, goal-directed behaviour for satisfying a financial need (e.g. merit pay increase) is generally evaluated by another person (e.g. supervisor). Fifth, **rewards** or **punishment**, depending on the quality of the performance evaluation, are given. Sixth, and lastly, the individual **assesses** the degree to which the behaviour and rewards have satisfied the original need. If this motivation cycle has satisfied the need, a state of equilibrium or **satisfaction** with respect to that **particular** need exists. If the need remains unsatisfied, the motivation cycle is repeated with possibly a different choice of behaviour.

This model will serve as the framework for our initial discussion of motivation theories. At the end of the chapter, we will re-evaluate and present a further development of the model.

## EARLY THEORIES OF MOTIVATION

The topic of motivation has long been of concern to both **managers** and **psychologists**. However, until recently, the emphasis and approach of these two divergent groups differed sharply. In order to gain a clearer understanding of how today's contemporary models evolved, it is necessary first to examine briefly the developmental sequence of both managerial and psychological models of motivation.

**Managerial Approaches to Motivation:**
The evolution of management thought concerning employee motivation passed through **three** relatively distinct stages, namely, traditional (or classical); human relations; and human resources. See exhibit 4-2 for the summaries of the assumptions, policies and expectations of each of these three stages of managerial approaches to motivation.

---

For this typology and its discussion, see, for example, Miles, R.E.; Porter, L.W. and Craft, J.A., "Leadership Attitudes Among Public Health Officials." **American Journal of Public Health,** 56 (1966): pp. 1990-2005; and Richard M. Steers (1984), chapter 6, pp. 131-159.

**Exhibit 4-2: General Patterns of Managerial Approaches to Motivation**

| Traditional model | Human relations model | Human resources model |
|---|---|---|
| **Assumptions** 1. Work is inherently distasteful to most people. 2. What they do is less important than what they earn for doing it. 3. Few want or can handle work that requires creativity, self-direction, or self-control. | **Assumptions** 1. People want to feel useful and important. 2. People desire to belong and to be recognized as individuals. 3. These needs are more important than money in motivating people to work. | **Assumptions** 1. Work is not inherently distasteful. People want to contribute to meaningful goals that they have helped established. 2. Most people can exercise far more creative, responsible self-direction and self-control than their present jobs demand. |

| Policies | Policies | Policies |
|---|---|---|
| 1. The manager's basic task is to closely supervise and control subordinates.<br>2. He or she must break tasks down into simple, repetitive, easily learned operations.<br>3. He or she must establish detailed work routines and procedures, and enforce these firmly but fairly. | 1. The manager's basic task is to make each worker feel useful and important.<br>2. He or she should keep subordinates informed and listen to their objections to his or her plans.<br>3. The manager should allow subordinates to exercise some self-direction and self-control on routine matters. | 1. The manager's basic task is to make use of "untapped human resources.<br>2. He or she must create an environment in which all members may contribute to the limits of their ability.<br>3. He or she must encourage full participation on important matters, continually broadening subordinates self-direction and control. |
| **Expectations**<br>1. People can tolerate work if the pay is decent and the boss is fair. | **Expectations**<br>1. Sharing information with subordinates and involving them in routine decisions will satisfy their basic needs to belong and to feel important.<br>2. Satisfying these needs will | **Expectations**<br>1. Expanding subordinate influence, self-direction, and self-control will lead to direct improvements in operating efficiency.<br>2. Work satisfaction may improve as a "by-product" of |

|  | improve morale and reduce resistance to formal authority- subordinates will "willingly cooperate." | subordinates making full use of their resources. |
|---|---|---|

*Sources:* Adapted from Miles, Porter, and Craft, "Leadership Attitudes Among Public Health Officials," *American Journal of Public Health*, 1966, 56, pp. 1990-2005.

**Exhibit 4-3: Historical Development of Approaches to Motivation**

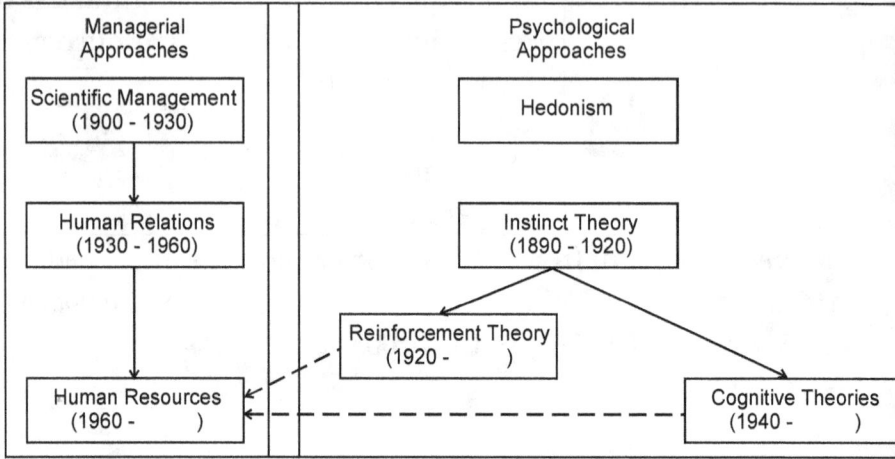

| Managerial Approaches | Psychological Approaches |
|---|---|
| Scientific Management (1900 - 1930) | Hedonism |
| Human Relations (1930 - 1960) | Instinct Theory (1890 - 1920) |
| | Reinforcement Theory (1920 - ) |
| Human Resources (1960 - ) | Cognitive Theories (1940 - ) |

*Source:* Richard M. Steers, Introduction to Organizational Behaviour. Second Edition (Glenview, Illinois: Scott, Foresman & Co., 1984), page 137.

**Psychological Approaches to Motivation**

Just as there has been an evolutionary process in managerial approaches to motivation, so too has there been a similar developmental trend among psychologists interested in motivation. This trend passed through an evolution of four stages:

(1)    hedonism;
(2)    instinct theory;
(3)    reinforcement theory, and
(4)    cognitive theories.

   As we shall see in this chapter, while psychologists originally approached the topic of motivation from a quite different perspective than did management theorists, the contemporary positions of both groups have apparently converged to a considerable extent. This convergence is shown in exhibit 4-3.

**Hedonism:**

The first coherent documentation of the principle of **hedonism** dates from the time of the early Greek Philosophers, such as Plato and Aristotle. It later re-emerged in the 18th and 19th centuries as a popular explanation of behaviour among such European Philosophers as John Locke, Jeremy Bentham, and J.S. Mill. The major tenet of hedonism is that individuals like to engage in various activities even though they may be unpleasant. Hence, more complete explanations of behaviour were needed. The first such theory that evolved chronologically was instinct theory.

**Instinct Theory (1890-1920)**

The first psychological **theory** of motivation emerged late in the 19th century as a result of the work of American William James (1890) Austrian Sigmund Freud (1930), and British William McDougall (1908). These theorists argued that a large portion of human behaviour was not conscious and rational, as suggested by hedonism. Instead, behaviour was thought to be largely influenced by instincts.

McDougall defined instinct as an inherited biological tendency towards certain objects or action. Included in the list of instincts were locomotion, curiosity, love, fear, jealousy, and sympathy. These instincts were thought to be the primary determinants of behaviour.

While instinct theory was fairly widely accepted during the first quarter of the 20th century, beginning in the 1920s it came under increasing attack on several grounds (Hilgard and Atkinson, 1967). The list of instincts continued to grow, ultimately reaching almost 6000. With so many variables, it became exceedingly difficult to develop a cogent explanation of human behaviour. There was no acceptable explanation concerning which of the many instincts would be stronger influences on performance. So, in the absence of a solid conceptual framework, it was difficult to predict behaviour. Also, it was found in various research studies that only a very weak relationship existed between an instinct and subsequent behaviour. Other factors were apparently also influencing behaviour in addition to the instincts under study. Finally, it was argued by some psychologists that instincts were not inherited, but rather represented **learned** behaviour. This last criticism was advanced by those who subsequently suggested a quite different theory of motivation: reinforcement theory.

## Reinforcement Theory (1920 – present)

Beginning with the early work of E.L. Thorndike (1911), J. Woodworth, Clark L. Hull (1952), reinforcement theory (also known as **drive theory**) emerged as a widely accepted, systematic explanation of behaviour.

Reinforcement theory assumes that people make decisions about their current behaviour based on the consequences or rewards of past behaviour. When past actions lead to positive consequences or rewards, individuals are likely to repeat such actions. On the other hand, when past actions lead to negative consequences or punishment, individuals are likely to avoid repeating them. This contention, known as the **law of effect** (Thorndike, 1911), emphasizes the role of learning on human behaviour. Past learning and previous **stimulus – response** connections are reviewed as the major cause of behaviour. Today, reinforcement still remains a popular explanation of human behaviour. This is discussed in the lecture on behaviour modification, an application of reinforcement theory.

## Cognitive Theory (1940 – present)

The most recent psychological approach to understanding motivation is cognitive theory. In contrast to reinforcement theory, where emphasis is placed on the influence of past rewards and reinforcements, cognitive models emphasizes future expectations and beliefs. That is, individuals are viewed as thinking, rational beings who make conscious decisions about their present and future behaviour based on what they believe will happen (Lewin, 1938; Tolman, 1959). Past behaviour influences these decisions only to the extent that the individual believes that past cause-effect relationships affect future events. Behaviour is therefore seen as purposeful, goal-directed, and based on the conscious behavioural intensions of individuals. **Significantly, it is this emphasis on reasoning and anticipation that sets cognitive models apart from other models of motivation**.

The influence of the cognitive approach to understanding motivation is pervasive and can be seem in several contemporary models of employee effort and performance. In particular, equity theory, goal-setting theory, and expectancy/valence theory all draw heavily from the basic cognitive model.

## CONTEMPORARY THEORIES OF MOTIVATION

In our earlier discussion of the definitional problems of motivation, we pointed out that there were a number of different ways in which people could interpret the concept of motivation. These different views provided the means for behavioural scientists to develop the three major categories of contemporary motivation theories: content, process, and reinforcement. These approaches are summarized in exhibit 4-4. We shall take up each one of these three categories at a time, and examine each of the various specific theories under it that are still of considerable relevance to both practicing managers and organizational behaviour researchers.

**Exhibit 4-4:   Contemporary Approaches to Motivation**

| Type | Characteristics | Theories | Managerial Examples |
|---|---|---|---|
| Content | Concerned with factors that arouse, start, or initiate motivated behaviour | 1. Need hierarchy theory. 2. Two-factor theory. 3. ERG theory. | Motivation by satisfying individual needs for money, status, and achievement |
| Process | Concerned not only with factors that arouse behaviour, but also the | 1. Expectancy theory 2. Equity theory | Motivation through clarifying the individual's perception of work inputs, |

|  | process, direction or choice of behavioural patterns |  | performance requirements, and rewards. |
|---|---|---|---|
| Reinforcement | Concerned with the factors that will increase the likelihood that desired behaviour will be repeated. | 1. Reinforcement theory (operant conditioning). | Motivation by rewarding desired behaviour. |

## (A)   CONTENT THEORIES

Content theories of individual motivation focus on the question of what it is that energizes, arouses, or starts behaviour. The answers to this question have been provided by various motivational theorists in their discussion of the concepts of needs or motives that drive people and the incentives that cause them to behave in a particular manner. A need or motive is considered to be an internal quality to the individual. Hunger (the need for food), or a steady job (the need for security), are seen as motives that arouse people and may cause them to choose a specific behavioural act or pattern of acts. Incentives, on the other hand, are external aspects associated with the goal or end result the person hopes to achieve through his or her actions. The income earned from a steady day of work (motivation by a need for security) is valued by the person. It is this value or attractiveness that we define as incentive.

The three most publicized and researched content theories of motivation are Maslow's need hierarchy, Herzberg's two-factor theory, and Alderfer's ERG theory. These theories have received considerable attention in both research studies and managerial application. We shall not take each one of them turn by turn, and carefully examine its major assumptions, contentions or postulates, its empirical tests of validity, reliability, and generalizability, and the extent of each theory's managerial application.

## MASLOW'S NEED HIERARCHY THEORY

Perhaps the most widely known theory of individual needs and motivation is the need hierarchy theory propounded by the American Psychologist Abraham Maslow. Maslow was a clinical psychologist who, in the 1940s, began his early developmental work on this theory among children with mental or emotional problems. Based on his observations, he attempted to develop a model of how the healthy personality grows and develops over time and how personality manifests itself in terms of motivated behaviour. During the 1960s the theory was popularised among managers and organization analysts, primarily by the work of Douglas McGregor (1960).

### Basic Premises of the Need Hierarchy Model

Maslow's need hierarchy model consists of three fundamental premises (i.e, assumptions), as follows:-

(1) People are wanting beings whose needs can influence their behaviour. Only unsatisfied needs can influence behaviour; satisfied needs do not act as motivators.

(2) A person's needs are arranged in order of importance, or hierarchy, from the most basic (e.g., food and shelter) to the most complex (e.g, ego and achievement).

(3) The person advances to the next level of the hierarchy, or from basic to complex needs, only when the lower need is at least **minimally** satisfied. That is, the individual worker will first focus on satisfying a need for safe working conditions before motivated behaviour is directed towards satisfying a need for achieving the successful accomplishment of a task.

Maslow (1968) argues that there are two basic kinds of needs: deficiency needs and growth needs. **Deficiency needs** are needs that must be satisfied if the individual is to be healthy and secure. "Needs for safety, the feeling of belonging, love and respect (from others) are all clearly deficits." (Maslow, 1954, p. 10). To the extent that these needs are not met, the individual will fail to develop a healthy personality.

**Growth needs**, on the other hand, refer to those needs that relate to the development and achievement of one's potential. Maslow notes that the concept of growth needs is a vague one: "growth, individuation, autonomy, self actualisation, self-development, productiveness, self-realization, are all crudely synonymous, designating a vaguely perceived area rather than a sharply defined concept" (Maslow, 1968, p. 24).

Maslow goes further to propose that people are motivated by five rather general needs and that these needs are arranged. A general representation of Maslow's hierarchy of needs is shown in exhibit 5-5.

**Exhibit 5-5:   Maslow's Need Hierarchy**

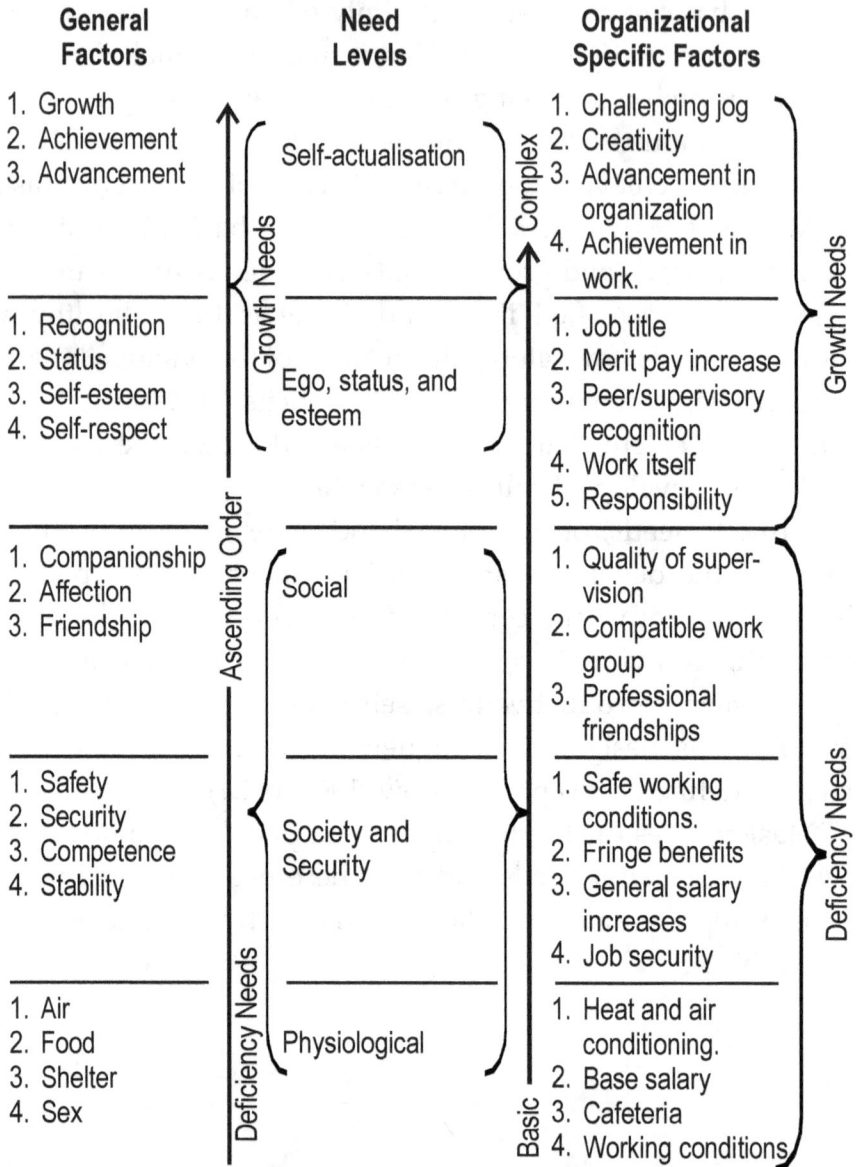

| General Factors | Need Levels | Organizational Specific Factors |
|---|---|---|
| 1. Growth<br>2. Achievement<br>3. Advancement | Self-actualisation | 1. Challenging jog<br>2. Creativity<br>3. Advancement in organization<br>4. Achievement in work. |
| 1. Recognition<br>2. Status<br>3. Self-esteem<br>4. Self-respect | Ego, status, and esteem | 1. Job title<br>2. Merit pay increase<br>3. Peer/supervisory recognition<br>4. Work itself<br>5. Responsibility |
| 1. Companionship<br>2. Affection<br>3. Friendship | Social | 1. Quality of supervision<br>2. Compatible work group<br>3. Professional friendships |
| 1. Safety<br>2. Security<br>3. Competence<br>4. Stability | Society and Security | 1. Safe working conditions.<br>2. Fringe benefits<br>3. General salary increases<br>4. Job security |
| 1. Air<br>2. Food<br>3. Shelter<br>4. Sex | Physiological | 1. Heat and air conditioning.<br>2. Base salary<br>3. Cafeteria<br>4. Working conditions |

General Factors: Growth Needs (upper), Ascending Order, Deficiency Needs (lower)

Need Levels: Complex (upper), Basic (lower)

Organizational Specific Factors: Growth Needs (upper), Deficiency Needs (lower)

*Source:* A.D. Szilagyi, Jr. and M.J. Wallace, Jr., Organizational Behaviour and Performance (1980), page 107.

## Deficiency Needs

Physiological needs are the primary needs of individuals, such as the need for food, drink, shelter, and the relief from or avoidance of pain. In the workplace, such needs are represented by concern for salary and basic working conditions (e.g., heat, air conditioning, and eating facilities).

When the primary, or physiological, needs have been minimally satisfied, the next higher level of needs, the safety and security needs, assume importance as motivators. These are reflected in the need for freedom from threat, protection against danger and accidents, and the security of the surroundings. In the workplace, individuals would view these needs in terms of such aspects as safe working conditions; salary increases; job security; and an acceptable level of fringe benefits to provide for health, protection, and retirement needs.

When physiological and safety and security needs have been minimally satisfied, social needs become dominant. These needs concern such aspects as the need for friendship, affiliation, and satisfying interactions with other people. In organizations, such needs are operationalized by a concern for interacting frequently with fellow workers employee-centered supervision, and an acceptance by others.

## Growth Needs

Ego, status, and esteem needs, the next level, focus on the need for self-respect, respect from others for one's accomplishments, and a need to develop a feeling of self-confidence and prestige. The successful attainment or accomplishment of a particular task, recognition by others of the person's skills and abilities to do effective work, and the use of organizational titles (e.g., manager, senior accountant, director or nursing) are examples.

Self-actualisation, the need to fulfil oneself by maximizing the use of abilities, skills, and potential, is the highest level of the need hierarchy. People with dominant self-actualisation needs could be characterised as individuals who seek work assignments that challenge their skills and abilities, permit them to develop and to use creative or innovative approaches, and provide for general advancement and personal growth.

To illustrate Maslow's concept, consider a newly graduated marketing student from a well-respected University in Pennsylvania who takes a sales position with a food products company in California. The initial interview trip plus the follow-up visit to locate housing have removed his concerns about base salary and housing (physiological needs). Because our new salesperson has a wife and small son, he seeks out information about such aspects as medical insurance coverage, use of company car, and so on (safety and security needs). The collected information, coupled with a long discussion with his supervisor about job security, have satisfied his concerns about these factors. The frequent interactions the salesperson has with his supervisor, fellow workers, and clients have proven to be most satisfying (social needs).

As time passes, the salesperson concentrates more and more effort toward doing his job as affectively as he can. Within three years, he has received a promotion to Sr. Salesperson and awarded the yearly sales award the last two years in a row (ego, status, and esteem needs). With the passing of a few more years, our salesperson begins to feel somewhat uneasy in his position. He feels a sense of needing to learn new things, to work on different projects, and generally trying to exercise more innovativeness and creativity in his work (self-actualisation needs). Subsequent years find our salesperson in the newly created position of General Manager of Product Development. Outside activities include active participation in local civic and charitable affairs, plus a revitalized interest in manufacturing stringed musical instruments in his garage workshop.

This example (which is an actual situation of an acquaintance of one of the authors) serves to illustrate Maslow's basic concepts. This is, needs are: (1) motivational, (2) ordered in an importance, or basic-to-complex, hierarchy; and (3) ascending the hierarchy is based on lower-need satisfaction.

Individuals move up the hierarchy by a process of **deprivation** and **gratification**. That is, when a particular need is unfulfilled (i.e., deprived), this need will emerge to dominate the individual's consciousness. Hence, a person concerned about physical safety will ignore other higher-order needs and devote all of his or her efforts to securing a safer environment. Once this is gratified, however, that need submerges in importance and the next need up the hierarchy is activated (in this case, belongingness needs). This dynamic cycle of alternating deprivation, domination, gratification, and activation continues throughout the various need levels until the individual reaches the self-actualisation level.

In summary, according to Maslow's basic concepts, needs are: (1) motivational; (2) ordered in an importance, or basic-to-complex, hierarchy; and (3) ascending the hierarchy is based on lower-need satisfaction.

An important point for managers to consider is that highly deficient needs, or needs that have gone unsatisfied for a long period of time, serve to cause such behavioural responses as frustration, conflict, and stress. Individual reaction to frustration, conflict, and stress differs from person to person depending upon environmental, organisational, and personal factors. These reactions to need deficiencies take the form of at least four different "defensive behaviours."

(1)    **Aggression** is a physical or verbal defensive behaviour that can be directed towards a person, object, or the organisation. Physical aggression can take the form of such things as stealing or equipment sabotage. Verbal

aggression can be the emotional outburst of an employee directed towards the supervisor concerning unsafe working conditions.

(2)    **Rationalization** is a defensive behaviour that takes the form of such activities as placing the blame on others or having a "take it or leave it" attitude. An employee may rationalise his missing a promotion opportunity by attributing it to poor supervision and/or inadequate resources, when in fact it was the particular individual's unsatisfactory performance that caused his missing a promotion at a particular time he was due for it.

(3)    **Compensation** concerns the behaviour of a person going overboard in one area to make up for problems or need deficiencies in another area. A person whose need for interaction with fellow employees goes unsatisfied during normal working hours may compensate by being extremely active in organization – related social, recreational, or civic activities.

(4)    **Regression** is a defense that significantly alters the individual's behaviour. After an associate professor has missed being promoted to the post of a full professor, he may change his behaviour from being friendly and open to being terse, highly task oriented, or temperamental.

These defensive behaviours can result from the inability of an employee to satisfy a personally important need. These behaviours are realities in any organizational setting, and it is the responsibility of the manager to understand the causes, and also help to find the relevant solutions to them.

Maslow in his later writings suggested that, unlike the other needs, gratification of the need for self-actualisation tended to cause an **increase** in the potency of this need instead of a decline. In other words, self-actualisation is a process of

**becoming**; this process is intensified, as well as sustained, as one gradually approaches self-fulfilment.

While Maslow did not feel that growth needs could be defined precisely, he did suggest some characteristics exhibited by individuals manifesting such needs based on his clinical observations. These include (Maslow, 1968, p. 25):

(1)    Superior perception of reality.

(2)    Increased acceptance of self, of others, and of nature.

(3)    Increased spontaneity

(4)    Increase in problem –centring

(5)    Increased detachment and desire for privacy.

(6)    Increased autonomy and resistance to enculturation.

(7)    Greater freshness of appreciation and richness of emotional reaction.

(8)    Higher frequency of peak experiences.

(9)    Increased identification with the human species.

(10)   Changed (the clinician would say, improved) interpersonal relations.

(11)   More democratic character structure.

(12)   Greatly increased creativeness

(13)   Certain changes in the value system.

Parenthetically, it should also be noted that Maslow (1954) also discussed two other needs in his early work: these needs are thought to transcend the notion of the hierarchy and, as such, are not included in the hierarchy itself. The two needs are cognitive needs refer to the desire to know and understand one's environment. Examples include the need to satisfy curiosity and the desire to learn. **Aesthetic** needs include the desire for beauty, harmony, and order in nature.

Cognitive needs are particularly important in organizations, as can be seen, for example, in attempts by employees to understand and relate to the tasks they perform and to be able to master tasks that are meaningful for them. In this sense,

Maslow's cognitive needs are similar to Robert White's (1959) notion of the **competence motive**. White, like Maslow, argued that individuals have a strong need to develop mastery over their environment. The importance of such a need becomes apparent in the recent efforts to redesign employees' jobs so that they are more challenging and meaningful. Job redesign experts hope that their redesign efforts will facilitate the feeling of mastery necessary to satisfy the cognitive and competence motives.

## Implications of Maslow's Need Hierarchy Model for Management

Maslow's need hierarchy theory has proved to be particularly popular among managers, probably because of its simplicity as a conceptual framework in the discussion of motivation. When it is applied to organisations, clear recommendations for management emerge. The theory suggests that managers have a responsibility to create a conducive work climate in which employees can satisfy their needs. Assuming that most employees have largely met their deficiency needs (i.e., they are free from hunger and threat and have established sufficient social relationships), managers can focus on creating a work climate that is aimed at satisfying growth needs. For instance, the proper climate may include opportunities for greater variety, autonomy, and responsibility so that employees can more fully realise their potential. Failure to provide such a climate would logically lead to increased employee frustration, poorer performance, lower job satisfaction, and increased withdrawal from work activities.

## Research on Maslow's Need Theory:

Since its development, a number of research studies have been conducted on the need hierarchy theory in organizations. From the standpoint of needs in motivation and satisfaction, a number of interesting results have been reported. For example, upper-level managers place less emphasis on safety and security needs and more importance on higher-order needs than do lower-level managers. Some would explain this as involving the process of career change and advancement. In addition, differences in need levels were found in comparing managers in small companies to larger firms, line managers to staff managers, and American managers working abroad to foreign managers. A number of observations are necessary, however, to further clarify the need hierarchy approach. First, despite some interesting and supportive research, other findings have raised a number of issues and criticisms about the theory and the viability of the five need levels. For example, selected data from managers in two different companies found little support that a hierarchy of needs existed. These studies identified two, not five, levels of needs: a biological level and a global need level encompassing the higher-order needs.

A second criticism is that an individual's needs should be viewed not in a static but in a dynamic context. Individual needs are constantly changing due to the various situations in which people become involved. For example, a manager striving to satisfy ego and esteem needs in his or her work may become concerned with job-security needs when adverse economic conditions have resulted in worker layoffs and terminations. Third, more than one level of need may be operational at the same time for an individual. The project engineer may be striving to satisfy a self-actualisation need while simultaneously being concerned with safety needs.

Finally, the theory states that a satisfied need is not a motivator. Although in a general sense this may be true, it is also true that individual needs are never fully or permanently satisfied as a result of a single act or actions. As we already pointed out, it is the nature of needs that they must be continually and repeatedly fulfilled if the individual is to perform adequately. If a number of needs are operating at one time, they would seem to contradict the idea of need satisfaction occurring in a fixed hierarchical order.

# CHAPTER SIX

# ATTITUDES

## (A)    INTRODUCTION

The nitty-gritty stuff which make up each individual's personality or behavioural system include cognition, beliefs, opinions, feelings, motives, interests, values, norms, attitudes, and behaviour. These, concepts are indispensable in social psychology because they are the elements which define the extent of ah individual's experience and behaviour in any social context. In fact, it is impossible to analyse and understand individual behaviour in society without these concepts, because it is they which sum up the personal history and biography, which account for a unique perspective on life and individual variations in social life. They are the psychological representations in the individual of the influence which society and culture have on them and vice versa. Each individual's tastes, preferences, manners, and morals are manifested and expressed through his cognition, beliefs, opinions, values, and attitudes.

This present chapter focuses specifically upon only attitudes. An attitude is an individual's basic psychological predisposition, orientation, or reaction towards any social stimuli - e.g., an object, or situation. An attitude is a psychological trait, and it is one of the primary factors which determine how and why individuals behave in whichever way that they may behave in society at any particular point in time. Therefore one cannot over-emphasize the importance of studying attitudes in social psychology. In fact, the concept of "attitude" has been a central one in social psychology since the birth of the discipline in the late 19th century. American social psychologist Gordon Allport (1935) described the study of attitudes as the major "building block in the edifice of social psychology." Two of the earliest researchers in the field, W.T. Thomas and Florian Znanieki (1918) went so far as to say that "social psychology is precisely the science of attitudes." While there is probably no expert who would make that assertion today, there is no doubt whatsoever of the continuing importance of the topic of attitudes in the discipline. William McGuire (1968) has succinctly summed up the current state of attitude research and analysis in social psychology as follows;-

> "This topic (i.e., attitudes) seems of such intrinsic fascination that we expect (it) to attract a high level of research in the future as in the past."

The various aspects of the subject of attitudes which shall cover in this chapter include the following:-
1)     Definitions of Attitudes
2)     Scope of Attitude Research
3)     Characteristics of Attitudes
4)     Types of Attitudes
5)     The Functions of Attitudes
6)     The Relationship Between Attitudes and Behaviour.
7)     Attitude Change.

## (B)     DEFINITIONS OF ATTITUDE

The concept "attitude" has a long, varied, and diverse history of usage in social psychology. It was first used at the early part of this century to mean a motor-mental disposition to action. Later it was used in a somewhat broader sense to refer to a specific or general reaction tendency which qualified and controlled the response to situations. Some social psychologists have gone so far as to use the term to cover the entire baggage of the inner psychological components of the Individual.

Nevertheless, most contemporary authorities in the field define "attitude" in a rather more precise and stricter sense to refer essentially to an individual's basic psychological predisposition, orientation, or reaction to any social object, or situation. It is the threshold lying between an individual's thinking and acting about anything or situation. The following popular textbook definitions reflect the predominant contemporary tendency to define attitude in this precise sense.

For example, Kimball Young (19:77) says that

(An attitude means) a predisposition to action, (it) is essentially afform of anticipatory response, a beginning of action which is not necessarily completed. This readiness to react, moreover, implies same kind of stimulating situation, either specific or general. Also, attitudes tend to have stability and persistence".

David Krech et al (1962:139) define attitudes as "enduring systems of positive or negative evaluations, emotional feelings, and pro or con action tendencies with respect to social objects." Gordon W. Allport (1935) defines an attitude as a "mental and neutral state of readiness, organized through experience, exerting a directive or dynamic influence upon the individual's response to all objects and situations with which it is related." Edwin P. Hollander (1976:139) states that "Attitudes are perceptual sets to respond to persons, things, and events." According to Lawrence J. Severy et al (1976:52) "an attitude is an orientation toward an object or set of objects, in one's environment." While Kurt W. Back et al (1977:240) state that "An attitude is a predisposition toward any person, idea, or object that contains cognitive, affective, and behavioural components".

All the above-mentioned authorities as well as most other contemporary social psychologists indicate that an attitude consists of three principal elements; an object, an evaluation, and a predisposition towards action. But Lawrence S. Wrightsman (1977:663) simply defines an attitude as "A positive or negative affective reaction of a relatively enduring nature to an object or proposition." He thus excludes the element of a "predisposition to action" from his definition of an attitude.

It may be observed that when "predisposition to action" is included in a definition of an attitude, it is presumed that attitudes influence concomitant or future behaviour towards the object. For example, if we know how an individual feels towards General Ibrahim Babangida, we should be able to predict how that person will behave when Babandiga appears in town or on television. Wrightsman agrees that predictions based on such knowledge are often correct. But he argues that the relationship between attitudes and behaviour is not always clear-cut. He gave the example of how in the 1968 United States of America's election, many trade union members were most sympathetic to presidential candidate George Wallace but ended up voting for Hubert Humphrey. Wrightsman then notes that "It may well be that in many instances one's behaviour determines one's attitude, rather than the reverse"; that he wishes to "de-emphasize the notion that a "pre disposition to action" is a pivotal part of an attitude"; and that he simply recognizes "that attitude's serve as ways for us to organize and categorize the information and feelings we possess about a number of topics."

## (C) THE SCOPE OF ATTITUDE RESEARCH AND ANALYSIS

The scope of the social psychology of attitudes is very wide and diversified. It includes studies of the varied and diverse types of attitudes which various people have about the virtually infinite range of things and situations that abound in the world - such as politics and politicians, changes of governments, the role of the military in governments tribal prejudices and discriminations, economic recessions and hardships, armed robbery, drug trafficking and use, smuggling, bribery and corruption, immorality and sexual promiscuity, etc. However, most of the current literature and concern in this specialty deal with the attitudes which some groups of people develop towards other groups of people. The specific types of groups involved differ from society to society. In the Western World, it is racial and ethnic prejudices and discriminations that are pervasive. In India, it is Inter-caste attitudes that abound. While in Nigeria and most other post-colonial African countries, tribal and colonial prejudices and discriminations are dominant.

Kurt W. Back et al (1977:240) observe that "what researchers have learned and may one day discover will, perhaps, help the diverse, people of the world live together in some kind of harmony". But unfortunately, most of the evidence available in the literature point to the contrary. That is, it appears that the more different racial, ethnic, and religious groups interact with one another, the greater is the incidence of the prejudices and discriminations that they display towards one another. Consequently, more research needs to be done in the area of inter-group prejudices and discriminations, in order to show precisely whether this hypothesis is true or false.

## (D)    CHARACTERISTICS OF ATTITUDES

Attitudes possess five principal characteristics, which may be regarded as the criteria for determining their presence or absence in individuals, as follows:

(1)    An attitude, like most variables of central interest in social psychology, is inferred from the way an individual behaves, it is not an observable phenomenon. That is, we never see an attitude directly. Rather, it is an underlying construct whose nature is always inferred from concrete human actions or behaviour. This inference, can be made in any one of several ways. For example, sometimes we observe a person interacting with an object of another person (e.g. stranger) and infer his/her attitude (toward that strange person) from that behaviour. Or, we might ask a person about the object (stranger); the individual's attitude toward the stranger would then be inferred from this behaviour, that is, from the behaviour of answering the questions as he/she did.

(2)    An attitude is learned (that is, an individual is, an individual is not born with any of his attitudes); and it is learned from one's experiences in encountering, perceiving, or dealing with objects, people, places, events, issues, or problems.

(3)    An attitude is an "organized" psychological "system" consisting of three principal component parts or elements: (a) cognitive, (b) affective, and (c) conative. In defining attitudes as "systems", we are emphasizing the interrelatedness of these three attitude components. When incorporated in a system, these components become mutually interdependent. The cognitions of an individual about an object are influenced by his affective

(feelings) and conative (action or behaviour) tendencies toward that object. And a change in his cognitions about the object will tend to produce changes in his affective and conative tendencies toward it.

(4)    An attitude is a specific and relative psychological trait. This means that individuals can and actually do hold as many different attitudes as there are different social objects or situations to respond/ react to. The range of attitudes is infinite or limitless. An attitude exists within a person in regard to every object, topic, concept, or human being that the person encounters. For example, people hold attitude towards their parents, children, families, ethnic groups, country, sports and games, jobs, educational qualifications, politics and government, public officials, wealth, poverty, marriage, religion, bribery and corruption, meaningful of meaningless life, etc.

(5)    An attitude is a psychological factor which predisposes its carrier to act or behave in a particular way towards the attitude's object or situation.

## (E)    TYPES OF ATTITUDES

There are many different types of attitudes. Attitudes may be classified into different categories, and specific types on the bases of certain common properties that they possess in common, such as the types of people who hold the same type of attitude, for example, the members of the same ethnic group (ethnic attitudes), racial group (racist attitudes), gender (sexist attitudes), profession (professional attitudes), age (generational attitudes) etc.

Secondly, attitudes may also be distinguished in terms of their being evaluated to be good or bad, or positive or negative. Good or positive attitudes are the attitudes which enable individuals to think, feel, and act favourably towards themselves and other people. In short, when people look at the positive side of life and relate positively to other people, such people are said to hold good or positive attitudes. In contrast, the people, who are always complaining about or blaming other people, things, or ideas, may be said to be holding negative attitudes.

Thirdly, attitudes may be distinguished in terms of the direction and purposes they tend and serve. The attitudes which enable people to think, feel, and pursue positive goals are called progressive and, civilized attitudes, such as the attitudes which enable people to think, plan, and work hard to achieve progress in their lives or to help other people to achieve success in their lives. In contrast, there are retrogressive, crude, and subversive attitudes, which are the attitudes by which some people think, plan, and work-hard to hurt, harm, injure, discredit, hamper, discourage, sabotage, and even kill other people.

## (F)    THE FUNCTIONS OF ATTITUDES

People do not just hold attitudes for their own sake or as ends in themselves. But rather, people hold attitudes for one reason or the other. That is, people hold attitudes because they serve as means by which they achieve certain psychological goals. In other words, attitudes person some important psychological functions for people. There are many different functions which attitudes perform for people, but the major ones are as follows:-
(1)    Attitudes help people to organize, simplify, and understand the world around them.

(2) Attitudes help people to protect their self-esteems, by helping them to avoid unpleasant truths and circumstances.

(3) Attitudes help people to express their fundamental and cherished Values.

(4) Attitudes help people to conform to their groups, norms and thus maximize the benefits that they derive from their groups.

(5) As a corollary of the last function, attitudes help people to adjust to their social environments.

## (G) THE RELATIONSHIP BETWEEN ATTITUDES AND BEHAVIOUR

One of the important problems in the study of attitudes is the relationship between attitudes and actual behaviour. Although all people have formed attitudes, a few find an opportunity to act in any methodical fashion in accordance with the attitude. The tribalist who hates people from a particular, ethnic group, may find himself marrying a wife from that tribe. A radical political ideologue who is usually critical of the bourgeoisie may find himself accepting financial assistance from a bourgeois. However, tribal or religious fanations usually always vote or support the political leaders from their ethnic and religious background. The above examples, show that there is no clear-cut relationship between attitudes and actual behaviour. In some instances, "people's attitude" lead them to behave according to their attitude. In contrast, in some other circumstances, there is really a big difference between attitudes and behaviour. For example, some people do not actually practise what they preach.

# CHAPTER SEVEN

# SOCIAL INTERACTIONS

## SECTION (A)

## INTRODUCTION

In this present chapter, we shall examine the forms of "social interactions" or "interpersonal interactions". The forms of social interactions refer to all of the various basic and elementary ways in which all of us individual human beings establish contact with, act towards, respond to, interact with, and exert certain positive and/or negative influences upon one another, as we seek to pursue and hope to achieve any one of our virtually uncountable different types of existential needs/wants in our every day lives in every human society across the whole world.

In studying the forms of social interactions, social life/social organization/social order/social fabric - in short, the totality of "man's social nature" - is seen up close, in microcosm, as a very dynamic, vital and fundamental aspect of our every day human life/existence/survival. The small-scale behaviour setting within which individual human contacts occur in any human society is the particular or distinctive centre of our attention in this chapter. The pattern of these settings, which is called the **micro-order** of human society, is based upon "interpersonal relations" or "social interactions", which means the process in which **individuals** act in awareness of the acts of others and also adjust their various responses on the basis of the responses of others. As a result, the study of the various specific forms of interpersonal relations/ interactions - that is the study of the micro-order" of any human society - focuses mainly on the particular behaviours/actions of only the very individuals themselves who are involve in such social interactions.

The study of "social interactions" is one of the major and very important specialties in social psychology. It is to social psychology, what physiology is to human medical science. In medicine physiology is the specialty which deals with all the types and dynamic processes of the microscopic biological activities of the human biological organism. Similarly, in social psychology social interaction analysis is the specialty which deals with all the various specific types and dynamic processes of the microscopic social activities of human society. Therefore, social interactions represent a very fundamental and important aspect of our total human social living conditions.

**Definition of Social Interaction**

Social interaction is the reciprocal influence which any two (or more) persons have on one another's behaviour, thoughts, and emotions, through symbolic and/or non-symbolic modes of expression.

## SECTION (B)
## TYPES OF SOCIAL INTERACTIONS

There are many different types of social interactions. The major ones are as follows:

(1)     Interpersonal Interactions
(2)     Face-to-Face Interaction
(3)     Focused and Unfocused Interaction
(4)     Strategic and Nonstrategic Interaction.
(5)     Symbolic Interaction

### (1)     INTERPERSONAL INTERACTIONS

The most elementary, basic, and pervasive way in which various individual human beings relate to one another, interact with one another, deal with one another, or influence one another, is when any two persons are involved in any interpersonal relationship/ interaction with each other - e.g., boyfriend/girl-friend, husband/wife, parent/child, brother/sister, lecturer/ student, leader/followers, boss/secretary, neighbour/ neighbour, friend/friend, car owner/armed robber, armed robber/ policeman, enemy/enemy, etc.

The term "interpersonal", simply mans between persons and does not imply that the relation/interaction is intimate; it may be quite impersonal. In fact, any interpersonal relation/interaction could assume any one or a combination of the various **qualitative dimensions** of human social relationship - e.g., it could be intimate or impersonal, cordial or hostile, voluntary in involuntary, positive or negative, permanent or temporary, etc.

### (2)     FACE-TO-FACE INTERACTION

Face-to-face interaction is one of special variants of social interactions. As the name clearly indicates, the major distinctive characteristics of any face-to-face interaction are that any two (or more) persons relate to, or interact with, one another in the presence of one another, in a direct, personal, and immediate way and manner. Theoretically, therefore, the persons who are involved in face-to-face interaction/relationship do not depend upon, or utilize the services of any form of **intermediary** factor, which is external to themselves - such as telephones, written messages, curtains, screens, masks, contact-men, advance-men, god-fathers/ mothers, big brother/sister, interpreters, etc. But instead, the major and most important emphasis in any face-to-face interaction is that the participants tend to predominantly utilize the interaction technique called "the personal touch" in influencing one another. The concept "personal touch" means that an actor" actress mostly draws upon his/her own personal ingenuity or charisma to influence another person in order to obtain some desired results(s) from him/her. Indeed, a face-to-face interaction is a potentially very emotive, sensitive, and effective way in which individuals can deal with, exert influences, and achieve (or fail to achieve) certain specific, urgent, and immediate results from one another.

The typology presented here draws extensively on the works of Peter L. Berger and Thomas Luckmann, and Erving Goffman - especially their works listed in the bibliography at the end of this textbook.

## Some-Important Characteristics of Face-to-Face Interaction

(1)     The most typical or ideal structure/format of a face-to-face interaction/relation is a **dyad.** That is, it mostly involves only **two** individuals. But it could also involve more people.

(2)     There is a predominant amount of direct and personal involvement in a face-to-face interaction. That is, there is a predominant use of the "personal touch" interaction

technique when individuals interact with one another in a face-to-face situation.

(3)     It encourages and enhances privacy in human relation-ship which is a necessary factor that enables some individuals to express certain very "private", "personal", or confidential" things to one another.

(4)     Communication is predominantly personalized, direct, immediate, verbal, full, explicit and reciprocal.

(5)     It involves and encourages maximum confidentiality, personal rapport, trust, belief, and credibility.

(6)     It encourages the attainment and/or the predictability of result(s).

(7)     A face-to-face interaction enhances the probability of the expression of any type of human feeling -e.g., emotionality, sentimentality and cordiality, as well as hostility and aggressiveness - in very extreme ways and manners.

Perhaps, among all of the different types of interpersonal relations/interactions, the face-to-face type is most liable to be given widely different and even contradictory kinds of interpretations. For example, two contemporary sociologists/social psychologists, Peter L. Berger and Thomas Luckmann, contend in their book, **The Social Construction of Relity: A Treatise in the Sociology of Knowledge** (1967): page 28) that -

> "The most important experience of others takes place in the face-to-face situation, which is the prototypical case of social interaction. All other cases are derivatives of it."

What Berger and Luckmann are saying in the above excerpt may be true to a large extent.  In fact, their view represents the popular opinion of many people from all walks of life to the effect that an interaction in the face-to-face situation is the most effective way in which individuals influence one another and quickly achieve some urgently desired result(s). For example, in this respect, let us say that one goes to, say, one's bank and attempts to cash a cheque in the normal way - that is, by posting it through the paying cashier at the counter. But, unfortunately, the cheque is returned to one uncashed, with either the Manager's or Accountant's "uncharitable" but inevitable professional remark of R/D (Return to Drawer) boldly written on the cheque, because there was insufficient fund in one's account. Let us any that one is really very urgently in need of the money, and as such one feels very visibly consternated and demoralized. Let us also say that a 'friend' is also around and he/she is aware that one is chafing under that very pitiable feeling of trepidation. That "friend" may nudge one and say: "Old Boy/Girl, why not go and see the Manager/Accountant himself/herself **personally,** and **explain** your predicament to him/her by yourself in a <u>personal</u> and <u>direct</u> manner? The 'personal touch' could be quite helpful in handling one's personal problems, you know."

Perhaps so. Assuming that one actually decides to heed that advice to see and talk over one's urgent monetary needs directly and personally with the Manager/Accountant. He/she may really feel sympathetic with one and help by approving an overdraft facility to one. But there is also the equally high probability that despite one's personal explanations and passionate pleas, the Manager/Accountant may still decline to oblige one. Therefore, using the "personal touch" is not an automatic guarantee that one will necessary achieve one's desired objective/goal.

Furthermore, there is also another widespread and misleading popular opinion about the use of face-to-face interaction which also requires a critical evaluation here. That is the view that it is most females (that is, women and. girls) who mostly like, and the actually mostly utilize the face-to-face interaction approach in dealing with and exerting certain emotional or sentimental influences upon other people (especially males). The major points in this viewpoint are:-

(1)     that females are naturally shy, and as a result they tend to prefer to express themselves much more effectively in the privacy of a face-to-face interaction;

(2)     that females can, and, if need be, best invoke their so-called special "feminine qualities" in order for them to be able to more easily and effectively influence males, and, therefore, quickly achieve their desired objectives/ goals, in the privacy of a face-to-face interaction. etc; etc.

There may be some general sense and truth in the above-mentioned "popular view"; but it is often over-exaggerated and misinterpreted by both males and females alike. Therefore, the following qualifications should be very carefully noted by students of social psychology, who should not accept any "popular opinions" on their face values alone.

Firstly, there is no available scientific evidence to show that females prefer to, and/or actually do engage in, face-to-face interaction more than males. There are equal chances that both females and males would engage in any face-to-face interaction, whenever they, as purely individual human beings, consider it to be the most appropriate way of interacting with one another.

Secondly, there is also no available scientific evidence to show that females are shier than males. Both males and females can equally display the same amount of shyness, depending on the types and the magnitudes of the factors, as well as the circumstances, which may warrant their having to display any shyness at all.

Thirdly, there is also no available scientific evidence to show that the mere invocation of "feminine qualities" (whatever they may be) by any female in any face-to-face interaction with any male would in itself alone, necessarily or automatically elicit the desired response and/or the attainment of the desired objectives/ goals by the female. Whether or not any female will achieve (or fail to achieve) her desired objectives/ goals therefrom will depend on a combination of several factors, which will include the qualities of the projected/preferred "feminine touch" as well as other extraneous factors, such as whether the male actor himself actually has the goods/services which the female actress desires, to deliver to her, etc.

As a matter of fact, the prevalent opinion/ belief that an interaction in the face-to-face situation can work "senders" or "miracles" raises certain pertinent questions as it also tries to answer certain other pertinent questions. For example, exactly what are the "important" kinds of "experiences" which some social psychologists like Berger and Luckmann say that individual can derive from a face-to-face interaction, which they cannot derive from other specific types of interpersonal interactions? How does one **measure** or **ensure** the validity, authenticity, or adequacy of the "influences" or "impressions" which individuals express to one another in any face-to-face interaction? And so on and so forth.

These questions and other similar ones about the real importance of face-to-face interactions have never been satisfactorily answered. That is probably largely because, as William Shakespeare has very succinctly said in his book entitled **Macbeth** -

> "There is no art to find the mind's construction in the face."

The main point which we are making here is that there is really no way to find out and ensure that whenever any two individuals interact in any face-to-face situation, they will actually express themselves in an honest, frank, comprehensive, accurate, reliable, or in any other useful/beneficial ways and manners to one another. That is because human beings are also very capable of either deliberately or inadvertently expressing themselves in predominantly unintended, and/or in superficial, pretentious, and misleading ways and manners whenever they are interacting with different people in face-to-face situations. As a result, people should not accept or make any categorical statement about the importance of any face-to-face interaction on its ordinary "face-value" alone, unless there are persuasive empirical data in support of any such claims.

On the whole, therefore, although the technique of face-to-face interactions may actually be a potentially powerful and effective way in which various individuals -both males and females - can, and often, do interact and influence one another, the science of social psychology does not yet have any reliable scientific toot/instrument/ mechanism to measure and/or predict, in any accurate/ adequate manner, the relative importance of the outcomes/ results which emerge from any face-to-face interaction (as well as the results which emerge from other types of social interaction).

## (5)    FOCUSED AND UNFOCUSED INTERACTION

Focused interaction specifically refers to the meeting of two or more people for the attainment of some common purpose, such as accomplishing a task, playing a game, or discussing something. In a focused interaction, the participants typically are acquainted with each other before the interaction begins, or they are in a situation which people are expected, and expect, to get to know one another.

There are many empirical examples of focused interaction in our everyday social life, such as the following ones:

(1)     When two or more students who are taking the same course decide to meet to do their homework together, in order, hopefully, for them to achieve a better result.

(2)     When two or more students decide to play any game(e.g. chess, ludo, ping-pong, tennis, etc) together.

(3)     When two or more political activists meet together and discuss any topical political issue, such as revenue allocation a newly announced state or federal budget, the creation of new local government council areas, the creation of new states, etc.

In short, the main distinctive feature of focused interaction is that the observed or observable pattern of interaction in question is actually deliberately and specifically focused or geared towards the attainment of some clearly anticipated objective, goal, or interest.

## (b)     Unfocused Interactions

Unfocused interaction is the opposite of focused interaction, to a great extent. In the unfocused interaction the participants come into face-to-face contact, but they neither know each other to begin with nor come to know each other in the course of the interaction. To disinterested observers, it might appear that in addition to not knowing each other, the participants in an unfocused interaction have no common purpose or interest in interacting. In fact, the participants themselves may not be conscious of any much purpose.

However, the most remarkable thing which gives unfocused interaction its own relatively distinctive characteristics and identity is that in any non-focused face-to-face interaction, the very fact that two or more people have come into some kind of face-to-face contact, that is, the fact of the mere presence of other people in any encounter - situation, would automatically, influence an individual's course of action in that encounter-situation, which would in turn influence the actions of the other people in the same encounter situation.

One very good example of an unfocused interaction is two completely strange people passing each other on the street. Let us say that these two people who have never seen each other before, pass by without exchanging a greeting, and that they also never meet again. Well, most people, especially non-social-psychologists, would say that there has not been an interaction between those two men that is, that neither of them has influenced the other. But social psychology argues that there has been interaction between them. Social psychology points out that if the similar behaviour of the numerous strangers who pass one another on city streets were not interaction, then there would always be uncountable collisions between such people on the roadsides of our large towns and cities. All those of us who are urban dwellers know quite well that although there are really some occasional incidents of mostly inadvertent road side collisions between strangers, uncertainly neither indiscriminate, nor the order of the day on our ditty streets. From the standpoint of social psychology, to the extent that strangers do not indiscriminately nudge and collide against one another when they pass by one another on streets and other similar public places, to that extent they actually, take some kind of cognizance of one another's presence, and as a result they actually engage in some particular form of unfocused interaction. One major proof of the fact that passers-by actually do engage in unfocused interaction between themselves is their mutual observance of traffic-routing conventions (which may be written and/or unwritten). For example, unless otherwise instructed, each person will pass on the other person's left. For one person to maintain a position in the centre of the sidewalk while passing another person will most likely be interpreted by the other person as an expression of mischief, ignorance, or rudeness.

Furthermore, if a stranger is passed, on the street and then seen again, perhaps later in the day, or even on another day, he will be fairly likely remembered. Thus, what has seemed to be a meaningless encounter has been carefully stored in one's memory.

Other similar examples of unfocused interactions include the harmonious/orderly behaviour of strangers in the waiting rooms of airports, railway stations, motor parks, the card-rooms of out Patient Departments of medical/health establishments, etc. The orderly behaviour of strangers in these and other similar places can be analyzed to show how each person's actions are influenced by both the written and unwritten rules which are socially acceptable as being appropriate in such public situation/fora. The momentary actions also greatly determine how these rules will be applied.

## (4) STRATEGIC AND NON-STRATEGIC INTERACTIONS

It was also the American Ervin Goffman, who coined and developed this specific type of social interaction. Goffman essentially intends it to supplement, that is to help to throw some more light upon the main body of the theory of symbolic interactionism".

Symbolic interactionism basically states that the people who are engaged in any interaction make deliberate and. conscientious attempts to weigh, define, interpret, and make appropriate and meaningful responses to the actions of one another. Goffman criticizes this theory on several grounds, but chiefly on the specific ground that it is so imprecise and general that almost all the many diverse forms of human behaviours can be explained or accounted for by the theory. At this juncture", we should realize that one of the major qualities of any good" or useful scientific theory is that it should be sufficiently "precise" so that it can be tested empirically.

As a corrective auxiliary device, the concept of strategic interaction" specifically seeks to emphasize the special significance of what Goffman called the **full** interdependence of the outcomes of an interaction". In a "non strategic interaction" two (or more) people may just come together, interact in a certain way, and part, without any indication of the direction of the outcome(s). But, in a sharp contrast, in the strategic situation one individual must-win or some how gain, while the other must lose. -For example, as in games and other contests, the winning is defined by the losing, and vice versa. In addition, each participant in the strategic situation must be aware that his gain will be the other's lose, for example, in soccer. Therefore, knowing all of these facts, each participant in a strategic interaction will make his very best efforts to outguess the next move of the other participant, so that he can move first, and also win. Finally, strategic interaction, unlike other interaction situation, necessarily involves a payoff, the nature of which will vary with the given situation.

Consequently, the concept of strategic interaction suggests needed specifications in the theory of symbolic interactionism. For example, that attention must be given to the conditions under which strategic interaction - that is, full interdependence of outcome, mutual awareness of this Interdependence, and a payoff - takes place and the ways in which behaviour differs between strategic and non-strategic situations.

## (5)    A Basic Symbolic interaction Model

Of the many models of communication that have been proposed, one of the more useful for understanding communication as a process is one derived from the field of social psychology. The model is called **symbolic interaction** and is illustrated in exhibit 12 - 12.

Symbolic interaction defines **communication** as the process by which one individual or group transmits meaning to others. Another way of defining **communication** is to view it as the process by which understanding is transmitted. As indicated in exhibit 12-12, when one person (the transmitter) wishes to communicate with another person(s) (the receiver), that Individual has some **intended meaning** in wind. Short of telepathic communication, however, he or she cannot place the message directly in the mind of the receiver. Instead, the transmitter must rely on the manipulation of something that exists outside of himself or herself, namely a symbol, to transmit meaning. **A symbol** is something that exists between

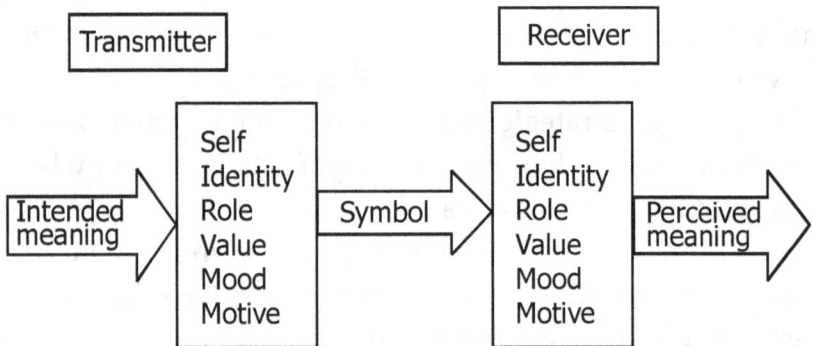

people and can be manipulated to exchange messages. Symbols have been called the objective or tangible side of subjective (or internal) ideas and meaning. Symbols take a wide variety of forms:

<u>Language</u> - Written and oral, constitutes a major vehicle for transmitting ideas.

<u>Facial and body expression-</u> Can be symbolic of messages a person is trying to convey.

<u>Clothing</u> - For example, a police officer's uniform that is used as a symbol of authority.

<u>Voice modulation</u> - Can be used to express surprise, anger, frustration, or fear, quite apart from what is actually being said.

<u>Religious signs</u> - Such as a cross, carry messages regarding one's religious faith.

Virtually any object or action can be used as a symbol in an attempt to communicate -among people, groups, and organizations.

If communication were completely successful, there would be a total overlap between the intended meaning and the perceived meaning; that is, the receiver would interpret the manipulation of symbol in a way identical to that intended by the transmitter. In reality, we know that communication within organization is rarely flawless. In fact, two communication processes intervene between two or more people and often result in imperfect communication: (1) symbolic manipulation (encoding) by the transmitter; (2.), symbolic interpretation (or decoding) by the receiver result in a **filtering** of the transmission and determine the **message** actually received.

Symbolic manipulation is the activity by which the transmitter translates his or her ideas into a set of symbols to be conveyed to the receiver. The activity is not simple. It involves not only the manipulation of symbols that transmit the message, but also the manipulation of symbols that establish the context within which the message is transmitted. Social, psychologists call this context a Self. It represents the transmitter and establishes his or her <u>identity;</u> the role in which he or she is communicating, his or her values, the <u>mood </u>in which the message is being transmitted, and the <u>motive</u> or reason for communicating. The Self then provides the context within which communication takes place. The same symbol can be interpreted in entirely different ways depending upon the context within which it is manipulated.

Symbolic interpretation is the process by which the receiver translates the symbol into his or her own interpretation or received message. Again, not only is the symbol itself interpreted but also the context within which the symbol is transmitted. The Self of the receiver is the context within which the message is interpreted. As in the case of the transmitter, the receiver's identity, role, values, mood, and motives influence the decoding and interpretation of the transmitted symbol. Symbolic interpretation, therefore, is a second filtering of the transmitted message.

A number of important conclusions can be drawn from viewing, communication as a symbolic-interaction process. First, the two-way process of filtering can lead to distortions and noise in communication. Second, the context within which communication takes place must be established and accepted by both parties before they can communicate, before employees can respond to communication, they must evaluate the source of the communication. Prior to this, they will neither receive nor be influenced by the communication. Researchers have found, for example, that the same message will be interpreted in entirely different ways depending upon the source of the message. Finally, symbolic-interaction theory suggests that to maximize effectiveness in communication, the transmitter must take the receiver into account very carefully. The transmitter should become as familiar as possible with the identity, values, mood, role, and motives of the receiver and should establish a Self or context that is compatible with that of the receiver.

## SECTION (C)
## GENERAL CHARACTERISTICS OF THE RULES WHICH GOVERN SOCIAL INTERACTIONS

Like any other forms of human social behaviours (e.g. group, organizational, or societal behaviours) which are always governed by certain social rules or social laws, social interactions are also governed by certain social rules and/or social laws. But unlike the rules/laws in those other more structured, organized and complex social settings, which are likewise complex, formal explicit, and written, the most distinctive feature of the various rules/laws which govern the various forms of social interactions is that they are usually **implicit, informal, ad hoc, unwritten,** and unpredictable.

A good illustration of the implicit and unwritten nature of the rules which govern social interactions is the phenomenon of "civil inattention" which is usually associated with the particular way and manner in which the generality of unacquainted people <u>react</u> towards one another in public places like streets, roads, lifts/ elevators, open markets, supermarkets, airports, railway stations, motor parks, public toilets, etc. Some of the most remarkable instances of the phenomenon of "civil inattention" occur in the Western or western societies - e.g. Western Europe, the U.S.A., Nigeria, Kenya, etc - in which there are implicit and informal rules limiting eye contact between persons who are unacquainted with one another whenever they come across one another in these types of public social for a. For example, when relatively strange people encounter one another in such public places, they are expected to glance at each other, but not long enough to suggest that the other person is an object of special interest. Thus, too much eye contact between unacquainted persons in public social settings in such societies can be quite embarrassing, and even offensive.

In traditional Hindu-Indian communities, eye avoidance is a manifestation of their caste system. As a result, it is the obligation of persons of high and outcaste statuses to avoid having unnecessary visual contact with one another. Similarly, in some tribal tradition African communities - e.g., among some Urhobo, Ezon, Isoko and other peoples - body avoidance is also a manifestation of their invest, adultery, and other sexual taboos. It is likewise the obligation of the affected relatives and non-spouses to avoid having unnecessary body-physical contacts with one another. Failure to conform to any of these and other implicit social rules which govern the various forms of social interactions in any of these as well as in any other particular cultural group across the whole world, results in the dissecration/ violation of the people's social rules, and as such some appropriate disciplinary/punitive/reactificatory measures may be applied to redress the malady.

Social psychologists conduct detailed scientific studies of inter-personal behaviours in various social settings in order to understand as precisely as possible the types and the effects of the specific informal, implicit, *ad hoc*, and unwritten social rules/social laws which govern how individuals behave and what they expect in any given social situation. Some of the available empirical evidence show that there are really different implicit social rules which govern different forms of social interactions, and that individuals wittingly or unwittingly conform to them. For example, in queues or waiting lines in any public social forum - such as cafeterias, banks, cinema houses, airports, railway stations, etc - there are specific implicit social rules/ social laws, which many people do not ordinarily bother to think about until one of them is violated, at which time it becomes quite clear how much the rule was an integral part of everyone's expectation within that situation.

On some occasions it may be acceptable or tolerable to violate some of these social rules/social laws, but their violation must be according to another social rule/social law which is given temporary precedence according to yet a third social law - and so on and so forth -depending on the social situation. For example, it is a fundamental implicit social rule/social law of queues, in many places, that each person on a queue will be duly served when his/her turn comes. But if, by some unforeseen chance the seats in say, an arts theatre, are completely filled up and as such the organizers in-charge can no longer allow more people to buy tickets and go inside the theatre, the remaining people on the queue who are thereby left stranded would most probably only feel disappointed but accept it as being mostly their own ill-luck, or their own inability to arrive at the place earlier than they did. But if, on the other hand, a person waits patiently in a long queue out of about two or more similar queues - in, say, a cafeteria, bank, etc - and then is suddenly told that that particular servicing spot is no longer offering the service he/she has been patiently waiting for, he/she may become highly resentful and even protest in an obstreperous and menacing manner, unless one of the supervising officers quickly and apologetically escorts him/her to the head of the queue of another functioning service-spot. The timely intervention of an official is necessary because going to the head of another queue by one's self would violate a second social rule (the first social rule prompting that violation being the organisers' unceremonious violation of the individual's "right to receive the on-going service". Thus, the role of the supervisor enables the organizers to properly make it clear to the people who are waiting on the other queue to which the affected individual is taken to stand in their front that a higher social rule of "fairness" is only being temporarily and specially invoked in that situation.

The crucial point which is being made here is that there are always certain important informal, implicit, often unspoken, unwritten, and *ad hoc* social rules/social laws which always govern <u>how</u> individuals should behave and <u>what</u> they should expect in any and all the different forms of social interactions which they engage in everyday in various different public and/or private social contexts in every human society, across the whole world. The most important meaning of this point is that individual human beings do not and should not ever behave <u>anyhow,</u> not even in such public places like motor parks, markets, airports, railway stations, cinema houses, streets and roads, cafeterias, etc; or in such supposedly very "private" or "personal" places like inside one's own bedroom, parlour, office, etc. But rather all human behaviours are shaped by written or unwritten rules/laws.

One of the major problems with the implicit, unwritten and <u>ad hoc</u> nature of the social rules which govern how individuals behave and what they expect in social interactions is that they are often **vague** and subject to <u>negotiation.</u> Whenever two people meet they have to work out for themselves the terms of their interaction, even though they will still be doing so within some **commonly accepted guidelines.** As a result, the micro-order of the interpersonal relations social interactions which occur in each human society cannot be properly understood without knowing the specific ways and manners in which the various individual in each society adapt to one another, and also in which they establish the forms and textures of their relationships/interactions. For example, it may be quite easy to describe in very general terms a female secretary's frequent and/or occasional to and fro shuttlings between her own office and her male Boss's own office. But the actual characters of the interactions and the special significance of the encounters for each of the two of them (that is, the female Secretary and her male Boss) depend on a combination of several highly diverse kinds of factors - e.g. on cues and nuances, on detailed ways of showing deference, maintaining distance, seizing opportunities, or overcoming barriers to communication and body contact, etc. Well, many of these and other "special" kinds of things which can also transpire between various individual human beings who relate to or interact with one another can not be effectively or comprehensively measured/explained/predicted by the social psychologist. Therein lies one of the inevitable major problems and limitations in the social psychological study/analysis of the various forms of social interactions.

# SECTION (D)
# THE RELEVANCE OR IMPORTANCE OF STUDYING THE FORMS OF SOCIAL INTERACTIONS IN SOCIAL PSYCHOLOGY

There are several very cogent and important reasons why social psychologists study and know as much as possible about any and all of the many different forms of social interactions which occur every day and in every walk of life, in all human societies, and in the whole world. However, there are <u>THREE</u> major and most important reasons, as follows:-

(1)     Any form of social interaction, is a potentially separate and independent small "social group" in its own right. As a result, like any other type of social group, any interpersonal relationship social interaction also therefore serves as a separate, independent, and effective social forum/context/setting in which any set of two (or more) individuals can act and interact with one another, and achieve (or fail to achieve) some of their desired needs/wants. For example, a lover gets (or fails to get) his/her desired emotional gratification, money, gift in kind or cash, promotion, good examination marks/ grades, delicious food, fine dresses, etc, from a "romantic", and/or "commercial", and/or "pragmatic" kind(s) of purely social interactions which he/she enters into with another individual human being - such as, boyfriend/girlfriend, husband/wife, sugar/daddy/sugar-girl, male Boss/female subordinate staff, male lecturer/desperate female student, and other similar types of purely interpersonal relations social interactions. Similarly, an armed robber succeeds (or fails) to get another person's property which he/she tries to snatch

from him/her in a "hostile" social encounter (social interaction).

In short, any specific type of social interaction is potentially an end in itself.

(2)    Social interactions are also fundamental to the science of social psychology because they are the building blocks of societies, communities, larger social groups, social aggregates/ categories, collective behaviours, and complex organizations, which represent the macro social contexts, and which are also major aspects of the total subject-matter of social psychology. Thus, for example, from a lay person's standpoint, any social group is composed of "just people". But from the social psychologist's standpoint, any human group is an intricate organization of different specific roles and modes of inter of interactions. For instance, in any typical African extended family group, or in any other social group, some individual members have authority over others, some are friends, some are enemies, etc. The more that is understood about leadership and friendship as general phenomena, the more any human group will be better understood. Therefore, the social psychologist may devote himself/herself to a detailed investigation of the dynamics of leadership as such, or to some other important aspects of social interactions.  The social psychologist studies the conditions which sustain any social interaction and the stresses and strains to which it is subject.  By so doing, social psychology contributes significantly to mankind's knowledge of the basic elements of all human groups/societies.

(3)    Furthermore, although the study of social interactions may concentrate attention on the relatively much more limited/restricted microscopic social elements or aspects of social life, the implications of such studies may be very far-reaching. For example, some particular types of social interactions, such as those involved in kinship, in educational establishments, in industries, in government and private-sector offices, in women's hair-dressing and general-body beauty sallons, in beer-parlours, in supermarket stores, in open markets, in the motor parks, in railway stations, in airports, etc, may be so pervasive and important that they actually characterize an entire society or country. Consequently, our knowledge of the predominant patterns of social interactions which occur in any society is an important ingredient towards our knowing the larger society itself.

# CHAPTER EIGHT

# GROUP DYNAMICS

## SECTION (A)

## INTRODUCTION

As G. Duncan Mitchell (1968: pp. 91 - 92) has aptly put it, the study of group dynamics, strictly speaking, is the investigation of the manner in which adjustive changes, occurring in a small social group as a whole, are the product of the changes in any part of the group. The term group dynamics has, however, come to denote the study of small social groups in action generally. Small group studies gained impetus during World War II, but may originally be said to have been inspired by the writings of C.H. Cooley and Georg Simmel. Cooley distinguished between primary and secondary groups. The former were defined as face-to-face groups which enjoy feelings of solidarity, groups that are productive of the moral norms operating in adult lives, or groups that reinforce these norms and the stability they produce in human society. Thus the family was regarded by Cooley as the main primary group, but others would include the work group, the club, the college fraternity and so forth. Secondary groups, on the other hand, are the larger aggregates like social classes, ethnic groups, etc.

Work on small groups gained strength during the last World War, the military organizations, of the Allies having come to appreciate the small group as a major factor in maintaining the morale and hence the military efficiency of the soldier. Pioneer work in this field was carried out by S.A. Stouffer in the U.S.A., many of his findings being published in <u>The American Soldier</u> (1949), and by a number of British psychologists employed in the war office, some of whom later helped to staff the Tavistock Institute of Human Relations in London. Experimental research work has been a prominent feature of small group studies. Kurt Lewin's influence has been strong in this respect, and together with R. Lippitt and R.K. White he carried out work with children's groups having different kinds of leadership: this was reported in 1939. Since then more rigorous experimental work has been done to discover the relationship between task performance and communication structures in small groups, notably by H. J. Leavitt in 1951 and by L.S. Christie, R.B. Luce and J. Macy a year later. These studies showed differential degrees of efficiency according to both the nature of the task and the type of communication structure involved. At the same time G.A. Heise and G.A. Miller also added some experimental refinement a with consequent theoretical improvements to the subject of small groups. These studies are reported and discussed by J. Klein in **The Study of Groups** (1956). Many other studies have been done, mostly by students of Kurt Lewin and many of them at the Centre for Group Dynamics at the University of Michigan at Ann Arbor, Michigan, U.S.A. Two major contributions to the theoretical development of Group Dynamics are those of G.C. Homans, who in his book **The Human Group** (1950), showed the usefulness of a systematic scheme of thought of a functionalist character by comparing various group studies, and by R.F. Bales, who provided a scheme for the observation and analysis of small group activities in his book entitled **Interaction Process Analysis** (1951).

The study of small groups has continued to be a major area of current research in social psychology arid the other behavioural sciences for at least three reasons. First, the group is a crucial element in social order in all human cultures and societies.

Groups serve not only as the focal point of social life, but provide an important source of direction to the individual for understanding social values and norms. Second, the group serves as an important mediating function between the individual and society in general. The individual may be able to satisfy economic, status, or friendship related needs through group membership. Finally, groups are less complex to study, examine, and experiment with than the larger organization.

Furthermore, the study and management of groups is especially important for social work practice largely because most of the activities and decision-making in the various organizations in which the social worker works are carried out within and through groups. It is through the actions of groups that many of the social worker's goals and objectives can be achieved.

For the social worker manager working in orphanage institutions, remand homes, prisons, hospitals, schools, community organizations, etc, the behaviour and performance of groups provide the primary mechanism for the attainment of organization goals. In order to provide for effective goal accomplishment, the social worker must be familiar with:

1. The process of influencing group behaviour towards goal attainment.
2. The climate for maximum interaction and minimal conflict between group members.
3. The means for the satisfaction of individual needs, which may I be different from individual to individual within each group.

On the whole, at the present time, the main aspects of the dynamics of small groups which experts and students study include the aims and objectives of groups, the sizes and structures of groups, leadership in groups, decision making and communication in groups, group cohesion, the influence of the group on individual members, the morale of the members of groups, and the like.

The application of small group theory and concepts may be seen in relation to work groups in complex formal organizations in commerce and industries, school classes, therapeutic groups in mental hospitals, and generally in social work settings.

In this chapter, we shall examine the foregoing aspects of the dynamics or small groups and relate them especially to social work contexts and needs.

## SECTION (B)
## THE DISTINCTIVE NATURE OF A SOCIAL GROUP

### 1.    Definition of Group

What exactly is a human group? Do the people who sit in the waiting room of the Head of a Department, the Dean of a Faculty, the Vice-Chancellor of a University, on that of an Honourable Commissioner of Education or Health, waiting for their turn to see the Boss constitute a group? How about the audience in a stadium watching a football match? Does the social unit consisting of a husband/father, wife/mother, son/brother, and daughter/sister constitute a group? What two bossom friends who are classmates in the school? As with the key concepts in other disciplines, it is difficult to arrive at a single, all-inclusive definition of a group that will be acceptable to all social psychologists. That is because there are many aspects of human groups. Social psychologists place more emphasis on some of the aspects of groups of the expense of the other aspects. For example, some of the experts say that the main idea behind the concept of a group is that all of its members must relate to one another in an observable and significant manner. Other experts say that it is the interaction among the members of a group that matter most. Some others argue that it is the shared concern and joint pursuit of the attainment of some goals by fellow members of any social aggregation that makes the aggregate to be a group. Finally, a growing member of social psychologists hold that the social group is an amalgam of all the above plus additional elements that make up a group. **Thus, a social group is any collection of two or more individuals who are interdependent; engage in frequent purposeful interactions, have a system of shared norms and inter-connected roles; there is pressure from other members to conform to norms; have a common goal: a** structure of communication and leadership; a modification of the individual's behaviour as a result of his belonging to the group; and the individual members derive satisfaction from their membership of the group.

Examples of social groups include the family, friendship groups, etc.

2.      **Group Formation**

Why do humans form and join groups? Some of the major reasons include:

(i)      task accomplishment;
(ii)     formal problem solving;
(iii)    proximity and attraction; and
(iv)     socio-psychological purposes

(i)    **Task accomplishment** is the primary reason for the existence of formal groups in organizations, communities, and the larger society.
(ii)   **Problem-Solving Groups**, like task accomplishment groups, are established for the attainment of some desired goal.
(iii)  **Proximity and Attraction:** Individuals also join together to form groups for proximity and attraction purposes.
(iv)   **Socio-psychological** group formation Usually comes about because individual needs can be more adequately satisfied in groups. Examples of such individual needs include:
(i)      Safety
(ii)     Security
(iii)    Social
(iv)     Esteem; and
(v)      Self-actualisation.

## GROUP GOALS

The aims and objectives of any group consist of the various goals which the members of the group work to get her in concert to achieve.

## GROUP COMPOSITION

Research on group behaviour suggests that the kinds of individuals who make up a group create a set of powerful determinants of group behaviour and performance. Many of the studies that have investigated the relationship between group composition and group performance have attempted to categorize group composition on the basis of homogeneous or heterogeneous characteristics. This break down classifies groups according to the extent to which the members' individual characteristics (e.g. needs, motives, orientation, and personalities) are similar or different. Each of these categories presents a different set of attributes that can lead to group performance. For example, in homogeneous groups the compatibility with respect of needs, motives, and personalities has been found to be conducive to group effectiveness because it facilitates group cooperation and communication. Although the homogeneity tends to reduce the potential for conflict, it also can create an over-abundance of conformity, resulting in unproductive group activity. In heterogeneous groups, the variations in individual characteristics help produce high performance levels and a high quality of problem solving because members stimulate the intellectual abilities of one another. The heterogeneity of individual characteristics in such groups can, however, create situations in which the potential for conflict is great.

A discussion of the relationship between group composition and performance would be incomplete without considering the nature of the group task. Studies concerning group composition have pointed out that the performance of groups depends to a large extent or the requirements of the task of the group, where task requirements are defined in terms of routine versus complex decisions and problem-solving approaches. Groups composed of individuals with similar and compatible characteristics (homogeneous) may be expected to behave in similar ways and will perform more effectively on tasks that are routine, and less effectively on tasks that are complex and require a diversity of problem-solving approaches.

On the other hand, heterogeneous groups can be expected to perform more effectively on tasks that are complex and require creative or innovative approaches to the problem, but less effectively on tasks that are routine and require a high level of individual conformity and coordination.

## GROUP SIZE

Group size refers to the number of people which makes up any group at any particular point in time. The size of a group has profound impact upon group dynamics, that is, the recurrent patterns of social interactions among the members of a group. For example, a large group has in its membership greater variety of resources for problem-solving than does a small group. However, the average contribution of each member tends to slacken off as a group becomes larger, and it becomes increasingly difficult to reach consensus on a number of issues confronting the group. Size is also a limiting condition on the amount and quality of communication that can occur among individuals. For example, in group meetings, individuals have fewer chances to speak when a group is large than when a group is small. And of course, the salience of the group to its members, that is, how important a group is to its members and how much the group affects them, is a crucial variable that is also related to size. On the average, the smaller the size of a group, the more salient it can become for the members, partly because of the abundant opportunities for face-to-face interaction that reinforces the sense of belonging shared by all members of the group.

Most small groups consist of two, three, four, or five persons. However the numbers can be core.

A two-person group is called a **dyad**, while a three person group, is called a **triad**. There are remarkable differences between a dyad and a triad. For example, the popular saying that "Two's company, while three's a crowd" is pregnant with some weighty meanings. For example, the existence of a dyad makes it imperative that the two members of the group must engage in continuous active participation for the group to remain alive. Because if either member withdraws from the group, the group ceases to exist.   However, a three-person group can survive the loss of a member. Thus, a member of a dyad is much more frequently confronted with All or Nothing than is the member of a larger group. Since either member can terminate the relationship and can thus prevent the completion of a task, a dyad often exhibits a high rate of tension; each person has to proceed carefully within certain limits lest the other party pull out.

Another important difference between dyads and triads is that the participants in a dyad cannot hide responsibility for events that occur within the confines of the group. In groups of three or more, one member can also reconcile conflicts between other members. If members of a dyad disagree, there is no insider to act as mediator.  On the other hand, dyads do not have to deal with the problem of intruders or spectators. Neither of the two needs to perform for the benefit of a third party; they do not have to worry about giving a third party "air time". Such factors, which are entirely due to the properties of size, have an enormous impact on our experiences in groups of all sizes.

The possibilities of a building coalitions and creating majorities also distinguish dyads from triads. A coalition and a majority are impossible in a dyad. However, a number of coalitions are possible in a triad, as the American sociologist Theodore Caplow persuasively argues in a book aptly titled **Two Against One** (1969). The power of majority over minority is particularly marked in a triad because the minority is always a single person who is left potentially isolated and vulnerable. Thus, a three-person situation opens the door to "divide-and - conquer" techniques. Perhaps not surprisingly, in most triads, members tend to switch coalitions from one disagreement to another in order to preserve the group's solidarity and viability.

Adding a fourth member to a group again changes things drastically. It opens up new possibilities for coalitions - for example two versus two; three versus one. As the size of a group grows, the number of possible relationships increases rapidly. As a result, a larger group tends to break into sub-groups.

Although the best size for a group varies with the task to be tackled by the group, researchers find that a five-person group constitutes the optimum size for many activities. For one thing, a strict deadlock is not possible with an odd number of members. For another, such groups tend to be large enough so that individuals feel able to express their feelings freely and to risk antagonizing each other; yet they are small enough so that the members show regard for one another's feelings and needs. Thus the size is a structural property of groups, and it has a considerable influence on the behaviour of members regardless of their individual psychological makeup.

## ROLE PLAYING IN GROUP

On any typical day when a researcher on group dynamics visits a family to observe the family members engaging in typical family activities, he will find that there is a flurry of activities. Every member of the family is doing something different - the grown-up female children may be busy trying to prepare food for supper; the grown-up boys nay be busy locking up the garages -and the gates to the house; the younger children may be busy answering telephones in the house and searching the television stations for a delightful programme; the mother/wife is hovering around the daughter(s) househelp(s) to ensure that they are getting the proper food ready on time for the supper; and the father/husband is sitting in the sitting-room, answering or making telephone calls, and telling the younger children in the suiting room to be careful with the television.

These different types of activities represent the division of labour in the family group. The behaviour that makes up any of these routine jobs are called a "role". Students of group dynamics have long bean interested in finding possible patterns of **role allocation** (assignments to separate jobs) and role performed by individuals in the group) in closed social systems like the family. Of major interest to the researcher are how the necessary jobs to be done by the members of each group are divided among them; how the division is understood by the members of the group; and how stable or consistent the constellations of role allocation and role performance are over time. Are the divisions of jobs in groups, always changing, or do they hardly change at all?   In other words, what place and what responsibilities does each person have in a groups? Consequently, group dynamics researchers are; **Does every group have a unique solution to the problem of finding appropriate roles for group members, or are there generalizations that can be made about what sort of roles can be found in any group?**

## GROUP STRUCTURE

Within any human group, some form of **structure** for group activity develops over a period of time. Group structure is the framework or pattern of relationships among group members that enables the members to work in concert towards achieving the groups aims and objectives. As shown earlier in exhibit 10:1, group structure is influenced by individual characteristics of group members, situational factors, group development, and previous performance. Our discussion of group structure will be twofold. First, a brief theoretical introduction to group structure is presented. Second, the structural dimensions of norms, status, roles, and group cohesion will be presented.

### Group Structure and Achievement Theory:

A theoretical framework that focused on group structure was developed by the American behavioural scientist Ralph M. Stogdill in his book titled Individual Behaviour and Group Achievement (1959). The theory is concerned with the individuals who make up group membership, the emergent group structure, the joint action of the group members, and the result of their interactions. The theory is summarized in exhibit 10-5.

The theory focuses on member inputs, mediating variables, and group output. Performances, interactions, and expectations are shown as **behavioural inputs**, which are attributes of individual group members. The effects of these behavioural inputs are exhibited in the form of group structure and group operations. The result of member inputs, mediated through group structure and operations, is group achievement. Group achievement is defined in terms of productivity, morale, and integration.

**Interaction**, a member input, is defined as an interpersonal situation in which the reaction of any member is a response to the action of some other member of the group. Interaction includes two or more persons, and consists of actions and reactions, or performances. **Performances** are responses that are part of an interaction, such as decision-making, communication, planning, and co-operative work. **Expectation** is the readiness for reinforcement that assists in determining group purpose, role differentiation, and group stability.

The three member inputs are not independent of one another. For example: performances and interaction combine to determine structure and group identity; performances provide the means by which an individual's expectations are reinforced; and interaction; and expectation combine to produce purpose and the mutual reinforcement of norms.

**Mediating variables** are the result of member inputs and include both formal structure and role structure. **Formal structure** is the result of the patterns of behaviour and interaction of group members, which in time develops differentiated positions in the group, such as status and functions. Status is the hierarchical relationship between two or more members, which determines the degree to which the individual members can initiate and maintain the goal - directed behaviour of the group. Functions specify the nature and extent of the contribution that each group member is expected to make towards the accomplishment of the group goals. **Role Structure**, consisting of responsibility and authority, concerns the pattern of group structure and focuses on the individual group member is expected to exhibit during the course of his or her involvement in the group. Closely related to responsibility is the concept of authority, which concerns the latitude or limits of performances to be exhibited by the person. In linking **formal structure** with **role structure,** Stogdill stated that the higher a person's status, the greater the authority and the nature of the person's functions are related to the degree of responsibility.

| Member Inputs (Behaviours) | Mediating Variables (Structural) | Group Outputs (Achievement) |
|---|---|---|
| Expectations | Formal structure<br>Functions<br>Status | Productivity |
| Interactions | Norms | Morale |
| Performances | Role structure<br>Responsibility<br>Authority | Integration |

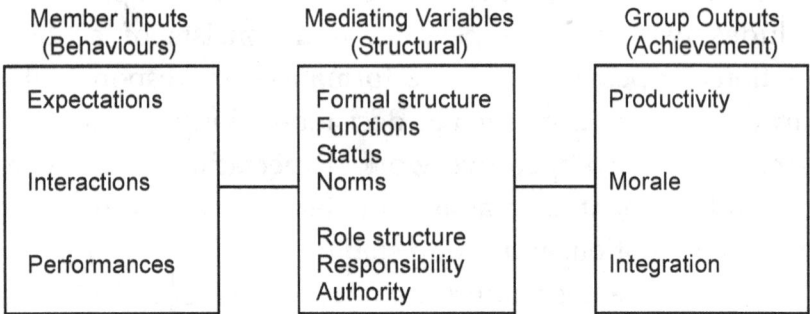

**Exhibit 10-5: Stogdill's Theory of Group Structure and Achievement**

Group achievement, defined in terms of productivity, morale, and integration, is the result of the interaction of member inputs (performances, interactions, and expectations) and the mediating variables (formal structure and role structure). Productivity represents the value (positive or negative) of the change created in the inputs on which the group performs its functions (i.e., the task). Morale concerns the affects of restraints on behaviour to group goal achievement in the attitudes of the members. Finally, integration involves the degree or extent to which the group can maintain its structure and interactions under stress. Stogdill implies that group integration is similar to the concept of group cohesiveness (to be discussed later in this chapter), which is determined by such aspects as mutual respect, trust, and member satisfaction with group behaviour.

Stogdill's theory of group achievement has been subject to certain criticisms because of the complex nature of the theory. However, the theory has been applauded by many researchers in a group dynamics because it provides a useful framework that not only is internally consistent with existing studies but can also provide the practicing social worker-manager with insight into the factors affecting or influencing group performance. For example:-

1. Groups place a great emphasis on goal achievement. Outstanding achievement serves to increase the status and prestige of the group relative to other groups.

2. Success in group activities acts to reinforce the expectation that further success may be attainable. Group morale is thus seen to be related to group productivity.

3. Group productivity is enhanced when function and status are clearly defined and when members in high status positions (leaders) maintain group structure and goal direction. Productivity is, therefore, related to leadership.

4. Because structure is determined to a high degree by the leadership of a group, and because morale is a function of structure, morale is therefore closely related to leadership.

5. Integration is facilitated when there is common agreement among the members of the group on the goals of the group.

6. The level of group motivation consists of setting attainable goals, reinforcing goal attainment, providing freedom of action, and providing sufficient structure for concerted action for goal accomplishment.

Many of the terms discussed by Stogdill - status, roles, norms, productivity, integration (cohesiveness) are important concepts for the for the study of groups. These concepts are examined in various parts of this chapter.

## LEADERSHIP IN GROUPS

Leadership has been considered as one of the most important elements affecting group performance. For the social worker-manager, leadership is the focus of activity through which, the goals and objectives of social work groups and organizations - remand homes, orphanages, mental institutions, old peoples' homes, youth organizations, etc - are accomplished. The leader has important influences on the attitudes, behaviour, and performance of members of groups and organizations.

Leadership has been studied and researched for a number of years, resulting in numerous theories and models. Like motivation, which we discussed in Chapter five in Volume one of our textbook. **Psychology for Social Work** (1997), no universally accepted theoretical framework of leadership has been developed. However, in this chapter, since leadership is not the main focus of the chapter, we shall therefore, touch upon only some selected aspects of leadership that .ire relevant to our discussion of the major topic of group dynamics, which is the larger concern of this chapter.

## Definition of Leadership

A.D. Szilagyi and M.J. Wallace (1990, page 277) say that **leadership is the relationship between two or more people in which one attempts to influence the other towards the accomplishment of some goals or goals.**

## Definition of Leader

C.I.D. Clark (1985, page 170) defines "leader" as follows:- **A leader is an individual who occupies a key position in a group, influences others in accordance with the role expectations for that position, and coordinates and directs the group in maintaining itself and working towards its goals. Generally, a leader is a group member who consistently exercises greater influence on the goals and activities of the group than do other members.**

## Leadership Functions

Leadership functions consist of the services that are provided by a leader and the needs that he fulfills for the group to which he belongs. Leadership functions include helping the group to establish its goals and define its tasks, maintaining harmony, serving, as a group symbol with whom the members can identify, and representing the group in its dealings with other groups or individuals. Although one or two members generally tend to exercise more leadership than others, the leadership functions may be performed by many different members at different times.

## Leadership Style:

Leadership style refers to the characteristic manner in which a leader exercises his or her influence in a group. There are many different possible leadership styles, such as "directive leadership," "group-centred leadership," "authoritarian leadership," "democratic leadership," laizzez faire leadership, "charismatic leadership," "task leadership," "emotional leadership," etc. The particular type of leadership style that prevails in any group at any part in time is influenced by many factors, including the situation in which the group is operating, the task or objectives of the group, the number of people in the group and the personal qualities of the leader.

## COMMUNICATION PATTERNS

Groups operate through communication among their members. Communication is not merely a matter of the language spoken and the types of printed or audiovisual material used to get across messages, even though these are important. Communication is also a matter of structure of the group and the physical and social proximity of the members. Any group must devise some way for its members to share their information. There are many possible ways of arranging the flow of communication, and possibly not all these patterns have the same effect on the work of the group and the relationship among the members.

A classic study of the influence of different patterns of communication in a problem-solving group was made by Bavelas (1953; Olmstead and Hare, 1978 pp. 102 - 110). Bavelas arranged groups of five persons in different communication patterns, such as the circle, the chain, the Y, and the wheel. In the circle, everyone had an equal chance to communicate with everyone else; in the other patterns the person at the centre had maximum communication and the ethers were restricted. Morale and leadership turned out to be closely related to centrality of position. Member satisfaction with the situation was greatest in the circle, where no one in the centre became the leader, production was greater but group satisfaction less. As an offset to its lower production, the circle was found to adapt more quickly to new tasks than the other patterns.

This is one example of how effective communication promotes the individual's satisfaction with the group and enables one to express oneself freely and to receive the impressions of others. A centralizing of communication focuses the attention of the group members on specific topics and promotes a concentration of effort. The implications for the organization of school classrooms and industrial work plans depend on whether major emphasis is on routine productivity or on developing flexibility and achieving satisfaction in the group situation. Research on the lecture versus the discussion method of college instruction, for instance, reports that students memorize as much even in very large groups with the lecture method (analogous to the wheel pattern) but that they have greater stimulus to do their own thinking in the discussion method (analogous to the circle pattern). These are a few examples of how small group research can help solve practical problems.

# CHAPTER NINE

# SEX ROLES AND THE CHANGING CONCEPTS OF WOMANHOOD

## INTRODUCTION

Since the beginning of recorded history, men have noted some fundamental differences between themselves and women. The sexes differ visibly in some physical characteristics. Do they also differ in behaviour capacities and natural inclinations? Are any such differences great enough that the culture must in some way take account of them?

To some extent, the answer is yes. Sex roles refer essentially to the idealized and general standards or expectations for the behaviour of men and women in any society. However, the division of roles between the sexes is not done arbitrarily, but rather there are certain important fundamental biological and macro religious, social, cultural, economic, legal and political variables which influence sex role allocation in most societies.

On the whole, the division of responsibilities between males and females in any society is not fixed but dynamic and variable. Sex roles can vary quite remarkably from time to time according to the combination of and the extent to which the biological, religious, social, cultural, economic, legal, and political variables operate to influence sex role allocation in any society.

In this chapter, we shall examine the division of roles between males and females in three historical phases, viz: firstly in traditional pre-industrial societies; secondly, during the early stages of industrialism in societies; and thirdly, during the later stages of industrialism, otherwise called post-industrialism in societies across the world. We shall also examine the extent to which changes take place in the allocation of roles between the sexes in various societies from time to time.

## THE BASES OF MASCULINE

## THE BASES OF MASCULINE DOMINANCE

One overwhelming evidence of men's superiority over women is that men have over time demonstrated in several concrete deeds that they are more pragmatic than women; and that men have sought and succeeded in being in-charge of women over the ages. Why do men seek to and how do they manage to succeed to command or control women?

### The Advantages of Controlling:

The advantages that men, and especially men in the upper social strata, have in controlling women include the following ones; first, subordination means control; if members of one group can reduce another groups scope of decision or freedom, then they can also gain their own ends more easily. Controlling women gave greater control, for example, over who is to be father of a woman's off spring. Having authority over their daughters and wives, they could keep them close by, ensure surveillance over then, and guarantee the purity of the family line. They could thus arrange family alliances for money, honour, or political influence. By controlling their wives and daughters, men could prevent the dissipation of family property.

Next, men at any class level simply cannot get done all that needs to be done in their small family economy without the help of a wife. These tasks include planting and herding, maintaining appropriate standards of hospitality, taking care of the children who are at once the adults' insurance for the future and their guarantee of family continuity, personal services, and validation as an adult. In most societies, a man without a wife is deprived of much that gives meaning to a social existence, but men control women and as such can obtain these advantages from them. Almost universally, to men it has seemed obvious that since women were frequently pregnant or nursing children they had to stay close to the hearth (fire-place in the house); and since they were there anyway, it was more sensible for them to carry out the range of tasks to be encountered there: gardening, preparing and cooking food, caring for children, sewing or repairing clothing, entertaining visitors, and so on.

A set of rules that defined all these as "women's tasks" would simplify daily living. By teaching young girls that this range of activities would be their destiny, men avoided arguments about who ought to do them, while they could also claim that only women were capable of doing them. Meanwhile, men were too busy at their own tasks to bother with women's work. Such a system or arrangement, once established, seems self-validating and is hardly open to challenge. It does work, and boys and girls are smoothly moved into their respective world without questions about alternatives. Grown men and women have generally believed, throughout the history we know, that the two sexes were almost as different as two species; it was as natural for women and men to follow traditional tasks, to acquire and exhibit sex-appropriate behaviour, as it would be for a goat to behave in a goat-like fashion. Consequently, few men or women would it have believed the charge that the two sexes are socially created, that sex role definitions are imposed, manipulated, and controlled.

Being in control gives more freedom. Men could go off for longer periods of time, farther, more often, and with less excuse, than women. By contrast, women were always on a shorter time-leach. The tasks of hearth and children cannot be neglected for more than a few hours. Men could, as they still can, refuse requests at less personal cost by claiming that urgent matters call them elsewhere.

These advantages do yield some satisfaction, some ego-enhancement; the male has commanded the centre of the stage, while women have been busily engaged in the work going on behind the scenes.

## SEX ROLE ALLOCATIONS IN TRADITIONAL PRE-INDUSTRIAL SOCIETIES

The term "traditional pre-industrial society" refers to a model or an ideal type that is essentially an abstract composite of features that are characteristic of pre-industrial and pre-modern societies. Such societies are characterised by small-scale institutional organizations. Thus, they have small-scale political, economic, legal, educational social, and cultural institutions. In particular, their economies are characterized by little or simple division of labour that hardly goes beyond age and sex; they are poor, homogeneous and subsistence. The main unit of economic, political and social organization is the family. The majority of people are illiterate. The standards of living, health-care delivery services, educational opportunities, etc are very low. Further, in traditional pre-industrial societies, such as virtually all African societies prior to their colonization by Europeans at the end of the 19th century, the bulk of the people's economic activities were in agriculture, past oral ism, fishing, and trading. Power, wealth, and prestige were largely based upon the ownership and control of farm lands, fish ponds, cattle, and trading sites and routes. Most of the people who owned and wielded the powers over those means of production were largely males; and they formed the class of aristocrats.

In the traditional pre-industrial societies, work role ascription was highly affected by physical sex differences. Men did the hard, difficult challenging jobs, such as hunting wildlife in the forests, grasslands, or in the seas and oceans. While women did work which could be combined with baby care - work which was repetitive, interruptible, and calling for no great physical strength. This had the effect of assigning most of the adventurous and exciting work to men and most of the drudgery to women.

We shall illustrate the above general principles of sex role allocation in traditional societies by examining sex role alloca-tions in a sample of traditional pre-industrial societies taken from different parts of the world, as follows:-

## 1.     Moslem Northern Nigeria

In traditional Moslem Northern Nigeria, the men are the bread-winners, while their wives are full-time house-wives, who stay in-doors most of the time. The men rear the cattle, farm the land, engage in both local and long-distance trading, and generally hustle and tend for their families. The "purdah" institution requires wives to live in-doors, cover their faces with clothes, and generally avoid having contact with other people, mostly men.

## Pagan/Christian Middle Belt and Southern Nigeria

In these societies, men and women work for the up-keep of the families. But while the men do the more challenging tedious jobs of clearing farmlands, hunting for bush animals, fishing for big fishes in the big waters, the women maintain the farms, sew clothes, do petty trading around the homes and villages, and generally provide auxiliary services for the men.

On the whole, the division of labour between the males and females in traditional pre-industrial societies was relatively simple and easy largely because of the simple, small-scale characteristics of traditional economies.

## HOW DIFFERENT ARE THE SEXES?

For centuries people have assumed that the differences between the sexes were inborn or "natural," that biology decreed different interests and abilities for men and women. Men were thought to be instinctively aggressive and women to be motivated to undertake child care by a "maternal instinct." Generations of husbands told their wives not to worry their "pretty little heads" about politics or business, and gallantly protected the "weaker sex" from the "dangers" of the world outside the home. But then researchers discovered societies in which men are passive and vain and women assertive and domineering, and other societies in which there are few differences between the way men and women behave. Consequently, social scientists began to seriously question the biological basis of masculinity and femininity. They asked whether anatomy was destiny after all.

Advocates (including men and women) of female empowerment began to argue that the differences in behaviour between males and females are learned, not innate. This view argues for the '"nurture" theory. By contrast, there are those who maintain that sex differences are innate. Those people argue for the "nature" principle. However, it appears neither of these two theories is provides satisfactory answers to all the questions that people ask about the differences in the behaviours of males and females across the world. But rather, it seems that some combinations of their views might address the unresolved issues more satisfactorily.

As we make our own contributions in analyzing and clarifying the various controversies about the differences between males and females in this chapter, it will be useful to make an important distinction between the meanings of two key concepts: <u>Sex</u> and <u>gender.</u>   The concept <u>sex</u> is used to refer essentially to the biological differences of males and females.

While the concept <u>gender</u> is used to refer essentially to socially agreed upon behavioural traits of men and women, especially those traits that have to do with personal identify, feelings about oneself, modes of dressing attitudes, and interests. On the whole, it is largely gender differentiation that results in cultural ideals of masculinity and femininity.

In the following four sub-sections, we shall briefly examine the important differences between males and females in four areas, namely:-

(i)     The Biological Differences,
(ii)    The Cultural Differences,
(iii)   The Historical Differences, and
(iv)    The Psychological Differences between males and females.

## (i)     The Biological Differences Between Males and Females

In most cases the anatomical distinctions between males and females are obvious at birth. Males and female human beings also differ in their sex chromosome and hormone make-up. Every human being has twenty-three pairs of chromosomes, threadlike bodies in each cell that carry within them the determiners of hereditary characteristics. Female cells have two X chromosomes, male cells an X and a Y. When sperm cells are produced, half of them have an X chromosome, half a Y chromosome. If an ovum (which always has an X chromosome) is fertilized by a sperm with an X chromosome, the child will be a female (XX); an ovum fertilized by a Y - carrying sperm produce a male (XY).

During the first twelve weeks the develop lag embryo is sexually undifferentiated. Differentiation into male and female depends on hormones, which are chemical substances that stimulate or inhibit vital physiological processes. The major sex hormones are testosterone and the androgens (secreted by the tests in males). These hormones initiate sexual differentiation in the fetus, and later, at puberty, they activate the reproductive system and the development of secondary sex characteristics, including breasts in females and beards in males. At some point the male fetus begins to produce testosterone, which inhibits the development of female characteristics. If testosterone is not produced, a female is born.

## (ii)    The Cultural Differences Between Males and Females

Social scientists have found considerable variability from one society to another in the behaviour patterns of men and women. This has made to be skeptical of claims that biological factors and the primary source of differences between the sexes. For example, American men have used the rationale that women are "fickle," "delicate," and "childlike" to exclude them from traditional male jobs. In contrast, the Tasmanians assigned to women the most dangerous hunting - swimming out to remote rocks in the ocean to stalk and club sea otters. The rulers of the African Dahomeyan Kingdom employed women as bodyguards because women in that society were believed to be especially fierce fighters. And among the Arapesh of New Guinea, women regularly carry heavier burdens than man do "because their heads are stronger than men's." Such substantial cultural variation among people of the world challenge our beliefs as to what is "natural" and "unnatural" behaviour for men and women.

## (iii)    The Historical Differences Between Men and Women

As we had argued in class when we lecturing on this topic of sex roles, the division of roles between men and women vary from time to time in most countries of the world as economic opportunities, political activities, religious practices and other relevant factors change.

## (iv) The Psychological Differences Between Males and Females

Psychologists have also contributed to our knowledge regarding sex differences. Probably one of the best-known psychological studies of the differences between males and females is the one by Eleanor E. Maccoby and Carol N. Jacklin (1974). They reviewed more than 2,000 books and articles on sex differences in motivation, social behaviour, and intellectual ability. After weighing the evidence, they concluded that the sexes do not differ in sociability, suggestibility, self-esteem, motivation to achieve, ease of rots learning, analytical ability, or responses to auditory or visual stimuli. However, Maccoby and Jacklin did find that the preponderance of evidence pointed to four differences between the sexes as follows: (a) that males are more aggressive; (b) that males excel at visual-spatial tasks; (c) that females show greater verbal ability (that is that women talk a lot); and (d) that males are better at mathematics (that is, that men are more calculative generally). Put in behavioural terms, that means that men are more logical and rational, while women are more irrational and illogical in behaviour.

## GENDER IDENTITY AND SOCIALIZATION

Right from when children are born in practically every human society, socialization agents such as parents, teachers, and other authorities function to transmit the social script outlining gender - appropriate behaviour to them from one generation to another. In the process, each human being acquires a **gender identity**, that is the view that each individual has of himself or herself as a man or a woman. It constitutes each persons inner experience or sense of himself or herself as being a male or a female.

The specific contents of sex-roles socialization vary from society to society according to their physical environments, histories, religions, economies, politics, and social and cultural factors.

## SEX ROLE ALLOCATIONS IN MODERN INDUSTRIAL SOCIETIES

The term "modern industrial society" refers to a model or an ideal type of society that is essentially an abstract composite of features that are characteristic of modern industrial societies. Modern industrial societies include all the societies which rely primarily on mechanization for the production of their goods and services. In turn this mechanization is based upon extensive use of inanimate sources of power or energy. The concept is also used to describe a society that has a high degree of economic development. An industrialized society is characterized by a specialized, coordinated labour force, a sophisticated monetary system for paying the workers and for purchasing the manufactured goods and services, and the technological means by which to achieve precise measurement and control of production.

The conditions under which an industrialized society can exist are primarily economic. They include new supplies of capital, new power sources, and skilled workers. Also important are formal education and a highly organized system between the suppliers of raw materials and the manufacturers. Historically, successful industrial nations have been those that have been large in terms of territory and possessed rich natural resources or have been active or international trade, e.g. the U.S.A., Western Europe, the U.S.S.R., Canada, Japan, etc.

The consequences of industrialization on a society include a constant demand for increased skills on the part of the worker, population growth; housing, public health programs, sewage, and transportation. Urbanization also leads to a breakdown of family life and communication and therefore a complex reordering of the society.

During the early stages of industrialization most of the available jobs are in the areas of construction, exploration, mining, and other heavy industries, and they are mainly men's jobs. But during post-industrialization more jobs are available for both men and women.

## CHANGING SEX ROLES

The Bible tells us that God created woman as an afterthought, to be a helper to man (Genesis, Chapter 2, verse 18), an arrangement which many men find very comfortable. Yet women's roles have shown continuous change. If we regard women's status as "high" when women have considerable independence, power, and choice, then women's status has varied greatly in tone - fairly high in ancient Egypt, low in early Greece and in the early Roman republic, higher in the later Roman empire, low again in the Christian era after the fall of Rome, low in the traditional pre-colonial African tribal societies, low in most Moslem societies in the Middle East and in Sub-Saharan African and high in post-industrial Western societies of North America, Western Europe, and Japan. What, then, causes the status of women to change?

## Factors in Sex-Role Change

There are many factors responsible for the changes in women's status from time to time and from society to society. However, the major ones are:

(1)   Declining sexist beliefs;
(2)   Changing work roles; and
(3)   Organized action.

## (1)    Declining Sexist Beliefs

Most educated people now agree that there are few (if any) innate sex differences in abilities and aptitudes, excepting for those which are purely physical. Even the physical differences are also shrinking. In many areas of athletic competitions, women are catching up with men, and may soon surpass them in some events. Thus, even the physical differences are partly a result of tradition and experience.

It is now widely recognized that "normal" sex roles are normal for only a specific time and place. Thus, intellectual under pinning for the subordinate roles of women has been largely demolished.

## (2)    Changing Work Roles:

The state of a country's economy at any particular point in time contributes in no small measure in determining the allocation of jobs between males and females. A relatively static, simple, subsistence economy that is characteristic of traditional pre-industrial societies, offers very few job opportunities to both males and females. While advanced industrial societies offer abundant and multiple job opportunities to both males and females. However the early stages of industrialization lowers the status of women by making men the primary breadwinners and women the helpers of men, because the major jobs are in the heavy industries, such as extraction, iron and steel, construction, exploration, etc.

But during post-industrialization, service occupations like marketing, advertisement, computerization, etc abound; these occupations do not emphasize muscle power and as such more women became employed, and many husbands find it increasingly difficult to keep their wives at home.

(3)    **Organized Action:**

Much of what we said about changes under Nos (1) and (2) above can be regarded as representing normal social changes in sex-role allocations that is they were not deliberately instigated and engineered by any group of people. However, that is not the only way in which changes have occurred in sex role allocation. Another important source of change is through organized social-political action by some interest groups. Important changes have actually occurred in women's positions in post-industrial societies as a result of the protests that were organized by feminist groups in Western societies. For example, it was largely as a result of the organized protest by feminist groups after World War I that women achieved suffrage after World War I in the U.S.A.

During the 1960s, in the U.S.A., feminist groups organized more large-scale, and sustained protests to challenge the various prejudices and discriminations which they alleged that the white date-dominated American society perpetrated against them. In some instances they joined forces with ether protesting groups, such as the blacks, students, and labour unions. This new feminist movement pursued three major strategies:

(a)    a legal attack upon all forms of formal sex discriminations;

(b)    an attack upon traditional sex-role socialization, and

(c)    an attack upon sexist institutional practices. And the new feminist movement actually achieved a lot of successes along these areas in American society.

## MARXIST ANALYSIS OF SEXISM

Marxist theoretical perspective is one of the perspectives that social scientists use for analyzing psychological, social, cultural, economic and political activities and developments in the contemporary times throughout the whole world. Marxist theory views sex inequality as an aspect of class exploitation, and asserts that sexism cannot be ended without a socialist revolution. But, unfortunately, socialism, which brings about economic equality, does not carry any guarantee of sex equality. Researches by various social scientists in virtually all the socialist countries of the world show that nearly all menial jobs are performed by women; the person driving the tractor was dependably male while the person with the hoe was dependably female. In the former Soviet Union and present Russia, women do most of the work in the fields, factories, and do most of the shopping, which is a very time-consuming task in Soviet Russia. Available statistical data do not give evidence that women's situations in capitalistic and socialistic countries are substantially different.

Two recent surveys conclude that women have lade greater progress in the socialist countries, especially in the former U.S.S.R., than in the U.S.A., but that in both societies women are heavily concentrated in pow-paid and low-prestige positions.

The Marxist rhetoric of sex equality, whatever its intent, has had the effect of "freeing" women to fill **two** jobs. It is possible that increasing the labour force, instead of achieving sex equality, may have been the primary goal of communist policy.

We know little of the status of women in the People's Republic of China. It is reported that virtually all women there work, with grandmothers often retiring in their early fifties to help with child care while mothers work. It is therefore difficult to know the extent to which Marxist sex equality argument has been carried into practice in China.

The Marxist theory that sex equality and economic equality are inseparable is contradicted to a large extent by the realities in the two of the world's largest socialist-communist countries - Russia and China. In short, the Marxist theory of a necessary linkage between sex equality and economic equality is not yet satisfactorily substantiated.

# CHAPTER TEN

# YOUTH CULTURES

## SECTION (A)

## INTRODUCTION

The concept of **Youth Culture** refers to the relatively distinctive subculture which consists of the values, roles, and general ways of life of young people in society. A society's total **culture** is generic, that is, it consists of several diverse strands that are called **subcultures**. There are several different subcultures that exist in the contemporary western and western-influenced societies, such as rural, urban, ethnic, counter, mass or popular, youth and adult subcultures.

This essay focuses upon youth cultures. It attempts to identify the various factors that are responsible for the emergence of different types of youth cultures; describe some of the different types of youth cultures; and examine the dynamics and consequences of the major types of the youth cultures that exist in contemporary societies, with particular reference to Nigeria.

## Exhibit (1): Typical Life Cycle Stages

| S/ No | (A) Life-Cycle Stages, With Approximate Ages | (B) Socialization Contexts or Situations | (C) Most Significant Others or Effective Socialization Agencies | (D) Primary Personality Traits Developed | (E) Emergent Personality Characteristics |
|---|---|---|---|---|---|
| 1. | Infancy (0 – 12 months) | Home | Mother | Basic disciplines | Affective gratification / sensorimotor or experiencing |
| 2. | Early Childhood (1 – 2 years) | Home, day care centres | Mother, father, duties | Basic disciplines, attitudes | Compliance / self-control |
| 3. | Oedipal period (3 – 5 years) | Home, day-care centres, kindergarten schs. | Father, mother siblings, playmates, duties. | Disciplines, roles, identities | Expressivity / instrumentality |
| 4. | Later childhood of latency stage (6 – 11 years) | Home, school neighbourhood | Parents, same sex peers, teachers | Disciplines, roles, identities aspirations, and skills | Evaluated abilities |
| 5. | Early adolescence (12 – 15 years) | Home, school, neighbourhood community | Parents, same sex peers, opposite sex peers, teachers | Identities, disciplines, skills | Acceptance / achievement |
| 6. | Later | Neighbour | Same sex | Skills, | Intimacy / |

| | | | | | |
|---|---|---|---|---|---|
| | adolescence (16 – 20 years) | hood community, school, home | peers, opposite sex peers, parents, teachers, loved one (wife or husband) | disciplines, identities | autonomy |
| 7. | Early adulthood (21 – 39 years) | Home, work-place, neighbourhood, community | Loved one (wife or husband), children, employers, friends. | Skills, disciplines, identities | Connection / self-determination |
| 8. | Later adulthood (40 – 59 years) | Home, neighbourhood, workplace, community, society. | Wife, husband, children, superior colleagues | Identities, skills, disciplines. | Stability / accomplishment |
| 9. | Early old age (60 – 69 years) | Home, work-place, neighbourhood, community, society, world. | Wife, husband, children, colleagues, friends, younger associates. | Identities, skills, disciplines | Dignity/ control |
| 10. | Later old age retirement age to death (70 + years) | House, neighbourhood, community, society, world. | Remaining family, long time friends, neighbours | Identities, disciplines | Meaningful integration/ autonomy |

# SECTION (B)
# DEFINITIONS OF KEY CONCEPTS

## (1)     Definitions of Key Concepts

## (a)     Life-Cycle

The concept "life-cycle" refers to the maturation sequence of human life from birth through death. The maturation sequence consists of several distinct stages of life. Both the numbers and contents of life cycle stages are physiologically and culturally determined. As a result, they vary considerably from one society to another. Nevertheless, the typical life-cycle consists of about **ten** stages, as shown in exhibit (1). Some societies may recognize fewer stages, while other societies may even recognize more stages, than the ones shown in exhibit (1).

## (b)     "Youth" or "Young Persons"

The social category that is generally called "youth" or "young persons" is also as much a product of <u>social definition</u> as of biological development. Although all individuals pass through a roughly similar sequence of maturation, cultural definitions of youth vary from society to society. Similarly, the recognition of both the distinct contents and duration of the youth category in the life-cycle stages differ widely from society to society. In short, youth is a concept that should be seen not simply in chronological and biological terms, but also in social and cultural terms.

Nevertheless, the typical youth category in most modern societies consists of the persons from later adolescence to early adulthood, that is the young persons of roughly from 16 to 39 years of age.

The young have become demographically, and sometimes politically, significant in the modern world. The age distribution of the global population shows a steady increase in the proportion of children and adolescents - largely because of the rapid population increases in Africa, Asia, and Latin America.

The young in virtually all contemporary societies receive more years of education than the young in the past. For example, in Nigeria, in 1959, only 10% of Nigerians completed secondary school. But today, some 60 percent do, and more than half of the secondary school graduates go on to some form of higher education (e.g. Advanced Teachers' Colleges, Polytechnics, Colleges of Technology, and Universities) - compared with only about 25% in 1959. One consequence of this increase in the education of the youth has been the emergence of a numerically significant youthful population that is

(1)     excluded from the labour force,

(2)     segregated from other age groups, and

(3)     concentrated together in large batches under conditions of high and intimate interaction.

Therefore, education has become a major factor in social change, and educational institutions have become the locus of unrest. The youth's major experience - education - emphasizes the ideal, and their lack of adult responsibilities frees them from those institutional ties and restraints that might have otherwise induced caution and pragmatism.

## (c)     Youth Culture

In every society in which the period of youth is perceived as a clearly marked-off stage in the maturation process, a youth culture has always developed. A youth culture may be defined as follows:

> A youth culture is the distinctive subculture in any society's total culture, which consists of the values, norms, attitudes, roles, and general ways of life of young persons in the society.

Many factors influence both the extent to which a youth subculture becomes differentiated from the other subcultures of a society's total culture, and also the specific contents of the youth subculture itself. Among such factors, the major one is **the age-based division of labour** in a society. The complexity of most modern-day societies makes the emergence of such culture almost inevitable, when young people are excluded from adult responsibilities for an extended period and are concentrated in specified locations (such as schools) their peers become the **primary preference group** for very many of them.

Social change can be measured by the degree of discontinuity between the culture of the old and the culture of the young. And wherever the young embrace cultural forms that are radically different from those of the established society, in times of rapid political, economic, or technological change, the implications are likely to be profound.

## SECTION (C)
## THEORY OF HOW YOUNG CULTURE DIFFERS FROM THE DOMINANT ADULT CULTURE

## 1.    Introduction

There has always been considerable cultural diversity in Nigeria. In the past, however, the society has usually stressed tribal or religious differences - as in the cases, for example, of the Hausa-Fulanis, Yorubas, Igbos, Edos, Ijos, Urhobos, Christians, Muslims, and the like. The general tendency throughout Nigeria's relatively short history has been for the dominant westernized and traditional elitist culture to absorb the others. But the clash of generations, with the concomitant emergence of distinctive subcultures of youth that often depart radically from the mainstream middle-class culture, is relatively new.

Some of the pertinent questions that sociologists ask about the newly emerged youth culture in the country include the following ones: What are the forms of youth culture in Nigeria today? Are they embraced by a minority or by the greater-part of the youth? Is youth almost universally opposed to the "establishment," and does this response take a uniform character? What is the basis of the cleavage between youth and adult culture? In essence, sociologists ask: **What are the forms and distinguishing features of youth culture in contemporary Nigerian society?** I will present a theory of youth culture in this present section (c), and then examine the distinctive characteristics of the major types of youth culture in section (d), (e) and (f), to test the validity of theory in section (C).

## (ii)    The Theory

Different sociologists have suggested and applied different theories to attempt to explain some of the forms and distinguishing characteristics of youth culture in contemporary

233

Nigeria, including the traditional functional, Marxist, traditional conflict, anomie, and phenomenological theories. All of these and other theories that have been used to explain youth culture in Nigeria and elsewhere have their merits and demerits.

However, one model that may throw more light in the differences between youth culture and the established culture in Nigeria is that proposed by American sociologists David Matza and Gresham Sykes in their article titled "Juvenile Delinquency and Subterranean Values" (1966). Their model was largely designed to interpret a particular form of youth culture that attracted considerable American attention in the mid and late 1960s - juvenile delinquency - but it still reveals certain characteristic features and values of contemporary youth that constitute the basis for their cultural divergence from conventional society.

**Exhibit (2):   Formal Values & Subterranean Values Contrasted**

| Formal Values | Subterranean Values |
|---|---|
| Deferred gratification | Short-term hedonism |
| Planning future action | Spontaneity |
| Conformity to bureaucratic rules | Ego-expressivity |
| Fatalism, high control over detail, little control over direction. | Autonomy, control of in detail and direction. |
| Routine, predictability | New experience, excitement |
| Instrumental attitudes to work | Activities performed as an end-in-themselves |
| Hard productive work seem as a virtue | Disdain for work. |

*Source:* D. Matza and G. Sykes, **The Drugtakers.**

According to Matza and Sykes, society is not only divided into horizontal strata based on class or status. There is also fundamental vertical distinction based on the value systems of the individuals within society, regardless of their social location. They said that two major competing value systems exist - the overt, official, or **formal** values of the society and its covert, unofficial, or **subterranean** values.  In the formal system are found such values as security, stability, and predictability. In the subterranean system, on the other hand, are such values as excitement, experience, enjoyment. See exhibit (2).

Within conventional society subterranean values are unacceptable except in limited and institutionalized forms - for example, during vacations and at sporting events, or at festivals. These occasions are clearly marked off from the ordinary working life of the individual and are seen in some sense as a "reward" for labours conducted in deference to the formal values.

Some people in society have great difficulty in ordering their lives according to the formal values, largely because there are cracks and strains in the formal value system. These people doubt the sanctity of alienated work and the validity of their leisure. For they cannot compartmentalize their life in a satisfactory manner their socialization for work inhibits their leisure, and their utopias of leisure belittle their work.

However, some groups are unwilling even to attempt this compartmentalization of existence. They are prepared to submit to the formal values, retaining only a part-time experience of the subterranean values until the pursuit of them becomes the distinguishing feature of their own life style. The young are particularly likely to experience the tension between the two value systems, because most of their experience has emphasized the subterranean rather than the formal values.

The effect of conflicting of youth and adulthood as they present themselves to the maturing adolescent could be quite dramatic. Society asks him to abandon his carefree life style in return for a new existence that offers little appeal – only a rigid separation of work and leisure, a reserved mode of conduct, an emphasis on the deferral of gratification, a concern for propriety, and the other restrictive patterns that seen to be the defining characteristics of mature adulthood in our society. It is not surprising that many youth refuse to surrender the life style they have and enjoy for one that offers few compensating attractions.

From the Freudian psychoanalytic perspective, the **socialization** of the child is aimed at bringing about a transition from the "pleasure principle", to the "reality principle", from the world of free expression and enjoyment to one of labour and deferred gratification. Each individual, having experienced the paradise of play in childhood, possesses the implicit memory of a utopia where economic necessity does not stifle his desires. The tension is particularly felt by the young as they stand on the threshold of adult responsibility.

## SECTION (D)
## TYPES OF YOUTH CULTURE

There are three bread categories of youth culture in both the contemporary western capitalist countries and the western-influenced third world countries, such as Nigeria, as follows:

(1) Conventional youth culture;

(2) Delinquent youth culture; and

(3) Counter-cultural youth culture.

### (1) The Conventional Youth Culture

Despite the problematic nature of youth as a stage of life in most contemporary societies (including Nigeria), the great majority of young people are **conventional** in their attitudes and behaviours. They adopt the roles that are expected of them by the wider society, attending diligently to their work and their responsibilities; they focus their enjoyment on those activities that are socially acceptable. They tend, on the whole, to be as politically apathetic and as unquestioning of basic <u>social norms</u> as their parents are.

Most conventional youth retain an <u>instrumental approach </u>to the world and experience feelings of guilt if they deviate too far from the formal values of their society.

The conventional young are considered a distinct youth subculture, because they also have their own heroes, jargon, and leisure activities, which are not shared by the adult people in the society. However, these differences seem to represent little more than the slight discontinuity between the generations that might be expected in times of social change. Otherwise, the formal values of society are scarcely challenged by conventional youth.

## (2) Delinquent Youth Culture

Delinquent youth culture refers to the ways of life of the young people who deliberately pursue subterranean values in a hostile society. Most of the youth who behave in this way tend to come from relatively poor working class family backgrounds. Delinquency among working-class youth is often a response to the feeling that the odds of life are heavily stacked against them - that is, that their school curriculum is irrelevant, that their future occupations are likely to be pointless and dull, that they will always be excluded from access to those things that are so highly prized in their materialistic society. As a result, their interests are focused instead on the here and now of life, on leisure activities, and on the search for "kicks", "excitements", or "fun". The search for the fulfillment of the subterranean values may take the form of overtly illegal acts (e.g., stealing, robbery, hooliganism, assaults, prostitution, etc.) It is very likely that some working class youth engage in delinquent behaviour because of a combination of reasons, including the following two reasons;

(i)     they lack the financial means to pursue the formal values of good living; and

(ii)    they have little fear of jeopardizing careers or peer group approval through "antisocial" acts.

Membership in a delinquent group can often be a useful element in the formation of personality. It may counteract feelings of insecurity, hopelessness, or boredom, and it may give the individual opportunities to "prove himself" by challenging the established order.

## (3) Countercultural Youth Culture

Counterculture refers to Bohemian lift styles. The counterculture is the nest recent and most controversial type of youth culture. It is found mostly in the United States of America.

It hardly exists in Nigeria and other African countries. Unlike the delinquent youth culture that arises among the young people who do not have access to the material rewards of their society, the counterculture emerges almost exclusively among the youth who are affluent enough to be able to enjoy the benefits of the middle-class life style. Bohemian life-styles are virtually restricted to the people who are affluent enough to reject the rewards that the less affluent continue to strive for. The countercultural young regard the middle-class life style and its comforts as somehow inadequate, even offensive; in a deliberate act of choice, they reject those benefits in favour of a life-style in which experience, expressivity, and self-gratification become the main-values. The key to this attitude is **alienation** - a feeling of being foreign to one's own environment, of separation from the values of one's culture, and a sense of the ultimate meaninglessness of one's destined role in life. In response, **personal autonomy** is asserted in matters of appearance, taste, values, and behaviour; materialism and rationalist, scientific approach that characterizes all industrial societies; are rejected; and there is an interest in <u>altered states of consciousness</u> – through drugs, religion, or meditation.

One further important element that is associated with the counterculture is rock music. Recordings and performances provide a medium of communication, a source of role models, and a force for social cohesion among the countercultural young.

## An Evaluation of Types of Youth Cultures

<u>All of these and other different types of youth behaviour represent different ways in which different groups of young people respond to the tensions that arise through the discrepancies that young people perceive between their earlier experiences and their anticipated later obligations</u>. All the

different types of youth cultures, stranded in a society that exalts the formal values of self-discipline and hard work, attempt to provide outlets for the continuing desire of their members to indulge the subterranean values.

In short, although we can talk generally about the existence of a major subculture called a "youth culture", it is also necessary for us to note that "youth culture" is not <u>homogeneous,</u> but instead it is <u>heterogeneous,</u> it consists of the different ways in which different groups of young people behave in society, such as "conventional", "delinquent", and "countercultural" ways.

However, it is also very important for us to note that all of the different types of youth culture are not necessarily completely distinct, separate, or exclusive of each other. Young people, like their adult counterparts, do not behave in certain clear-out and fixed ways that follow the formal-subterranean distinction all the time. For an ardent leftist youth can be otherwise conventional in his adherence to formal cultural norms, and some young people who have no political interests whatsoever may still reject every significant value of their society. Nevertheless, we may recognize a minimal distinction between the young people who are out to change society through commitment and action and other young people who avoid protest and prefer to withdraw into an intensified subjectivity. In reality, this distinction is also not a hard-and-fast one.

Although youth in the contemporary Western and Western-influenced Third World countries, like Nigeria, are in an unprecedented state of ferment, the majority of them remain socially stabilized within the context of their established society. Yet there are certain times when youth may perceive a common interest and interdependence that over-rides their individual and sectional differences. One striking recent example was the political protest of American youth against the Vietnam war. In such an occasion the unanimity of thought and action among the young was broader, deeper, more intense, and quicker to emerge than among adults.

## SECTION (E)
## POPULAR YOUTH CULTURE IN NIGERIA

Popular youth culture refers to the leisure behaviour of young persons in society. That is, the various pastimes, or entertainments which mostly the youth engage in when they are not working (e.g., studying their books, or learning whatever trade or skill) are called "popular youth culture". Popular youth culture includes all forms of youth entertainment in sound, sight, and the printed word. Young people in Nigeria spend about four to six hours daily watching a television or listening to the radio or to some other form of music player (e.g. a phonograph, etc.) The amount of time and money alone that the youth spend on popular culture clearly shows that it is quite an important aspect of Nigerian youth culture.

The average Nigerian youth (like their counterparts in other westernized countries) voluntarily devotes his time to popular culture, whereas his enthusiasms for and commitment to study, work, religion, and other activities may be quite slight. For example, most young people go to school to learn books only because they have to, but they patronize pop culture because of choice and in some cases habit. They may choose to see a movie, watch television, listen to a stereo set, or read a novel. On weekends, they may travel to discos, festivals, picnics, or attend a concert or a sport event (e.g., football).

Popular youth culture is the entertainment subdivision of youth culture. It lacks coercion arid any long-standing pattern or uniformity. Change, both expected and unexpected, is the rule rather than the exception in popular culture. Popular culture is entertainment that people support at any particular moment. There is **no** consistent style or form that makes-up popular culture. Popular culture is immediate. It has no tradition. It can be an oversight sensation or a lasting style that ebbs and flows over several decades. Popular culture does not require pre-training or preparation. Popular culture exists because it has audiences <u>large enough to support it.</u> This audience may lend its support for a short or a long time.

Popular culture events occur in <u>three</u> basic forms: **fads, crazes,** and **trends.** These forms are distinguished by the amount of time and degree of intensity or sensationality in which people patronize them.

For definitions and descriptions of fads and crazes, see C.l.D. Clark, <u>Collective Behaviour and Social Movements</u> (1985: pp. 68-81).

A <u>trend</u> is a long-term fashion (fad or craze) that does not change quickly. Musical styles, movie formats, hair or dressing styles, book themes, and the like, are all subject to trends. For example, reggae music which has all but dominated the sphere of popular youth music in Nigeria from the mid-1970s to the present, is a trend. Likewise romantic movies and novels.

In short, popular youth culture in Nigeria, like in the Western countries, is largely made up of fads, crazes, and trends. Stages are determined by the patronizers' fancy. They animate as much and last as long as their patronizers support them. Time is an important factor in popular culture. Another is economic support.

In conclusion, sociologists study popular youth culture in order to understand the various ways in which young people spend their leisure time in any society, such as in Nigeria, or in the United States of America.

# CHAPTER ELEVEN

# ABNORMAL BEHAVIOUR

## SECTION (A)

## INTRODUCTION

The social psychologist is a person who has been trained to know how to identify, analyse, and help to solve varieties of psychological and social problems which affect individuals, social groups, and communities. While psychology is the academic and professional discipline which uses scientific methods to study, analyse, and generate technical information about the behaviours and related mental and physical processes of individuals. Thus psychologists possess some relevant knowledge, skills, and abilities to identify normal as well as abnormal behaviours, analyse, explain, and predict abnormal behaviours, as well as considerable expertise to control them.

The social psychologist needs all the technical information and practical techniques that he can get to enable him to help the various people who are suffering from different types of abnormal behaviour. The psychology of abnormal behaviour generates such bodies of technical information that are useful to social psychologist. In addition, the social psychologist also needs to learn some of psychology's therapeutic techniques for controlling different types of abnormal behaviour.

The foregoing are among the major goals that we shall attempt to pursue and achieve in this chapter. To enable us to achieve those goals, we shall in section (B) pose and find appropriate answers to the question: What is abnormal behaviour? In section (C) we shall examine the historical views about abnormal behaviour. In section (D) we shall briefly examine the current major explanations which psychology has offered for abnormal behaviour.

In section (E) we shall examine seven major categories and their various specific types of abnormal behaviour which psychologists usually study, such as Anxiety Disorders, Somatoform Disorders, Psychophysical Disorders, Dissociative Disorders, Affective Disorders, Personality Disorders, and Schizophrenic Disorders.

# SECTION (B)
# WHAT IS ABNORMAL BEHAVIOUR?

The study of abnormal behaviour is a very important aspect of the psychological study of behaviour and mental processes. What is abnormal behaviour? There is no one standard definition of abnormal behaviour that would be readily acceptable to all the different people who are concerned about abnormal behaviour, because different professionals use different standards and systems of values to define abnormal behaviour. The standards and systems of values include society's, the individual's, the mental health professional's, etc. See, for example, the society's, individual's and the mental health professional's different viewpoints about mental health summarized in table one.

To a large extent, psychologists use **intrapersonal standards of normality** – that is, they try to evaluate people in terms of their own lives. On the whole there are **four** criteria which most psychologists would use to identify abnormal behaviour as follows:-

(1)  Distorted perception of reality;

(2)  Carrying out an inappropriate behaviour;

(3)  Discomfort or impaired ability to cope with life's demands; and that

(4)  The behaviour constitutes danger – to oneself or to others.

**Table 1: Viewpoint** ......................................

|  | Standards/Values | Measures |
|---|---|---|
| Society | Orderly world in which people assume responsibility for their assigned social roles | Observations of behaviour, extent to which a person fulfils society's expectations |

| | (e.g., bread-winner, parent), conform to prevailing mores, and meet situational requirements. | and measures up to prevailing standards. |
|---|---|---|
| Individual | Happiness, gratification needs. | Subjective perceptions of self-esteem, acceptance, and well being. |
| Mental health professional | Sound personality structure characterized by growth, development, autonomy, environmental mastery, ability to cope with stress, adaptation. | Clinical judgement, aided by behavioural observations and psychological tests of such variables as self-concepts, sense of identity, balance of psychic forces, unified outlook on life, resistance to stress, self-regulation, ability to cope with reality, absence of mental and behavioural symptoms, adequacy in love, work, and play, adequacy in interpersonal relationships. |

*Source:* Adapted from Strupp & Hadley. Copyright 1977 by the American Psychological Association. Adapted by permission of the author.

## SECTION (C)
## SOME HISTORICAL VIEWS ABOUT ABNORMAL BEHAVIOUR

Long long times ago during our traditional times, our forefathers' world views were dominated by beliefs in supernatural powers, witchcraft, sorcery, and the like. Such beliefs were used by our forefathers to explain virtually everything – good or bad – that happened in our traditional societies, such as madness, violent behaviour, or mere eccentricity. Abnormal behaviour was often considered the work of demons; the disturbed person was often believed to be a witch or possessed by the devil. Exorcisms, from mild to hair-raising, were performed or abnormal people, and a number of unfortunate people endured horrifying torture, while some others died.

However, not all mentally disturbed people were persecuted or tortured. Since the extended family was the major social group that discharged most responsibilities to individuals, some cases of abnormal people were taken care of by their families. Such abnormal people were confined in private asylums, where they were treated by diviners, juju/medicine experts, and generally looked after by adult relations. Some of such abnormal people recovered, while others did not recover until they died.

With the advent of the British colonization of Nigeria and the subsequent westernisation and modernization that they introduced into the country new western scientific concepts, theories, and methods of controlling abnormal behaviours were likewise introduced into Nigeria and all the other colonized African countries since the beginning of the 20th century.

## SECTION (D)
## CURRENT VIEWS ABOUT ABNORMAL BEHAVIOUR

In the present contemporary times, there are many varied perspectives about abnormal behaviour, each of which has substantial followers. In this sub-section, we shall present the high-lights of the view points which some of the schools of thought in psychology have offered about abnormal behaviour.

1.　　**The Psychoanalytic Model:**

The psychoanalytic perspective on abnormal behaviour was developed by Sigmund Freud and his followers. According to this model, abnormal behaviours are symbolic expressions of unconscious internal conflicts of the individual. For example, a man who behaves towards women in a violent way may be unconsciously expressing rage against his mother for being unaffectionate towards him during his childhood. The psychoanalytic model argues that people must become aware that the source of their problems lies in their childhood and infancy before they can resolve these problems effectively.

2.　　**The Behavioural Model**

According to the behavioural model, abnormal behaviour, like normal behaviour, is the result of learning. Fear, anxiety, frigidity, and other forms of abnormal behaviours, are learned and they can be unlearned using the same principles of learning, with the probing of an analyst or the use of drugs.

3.　　**The Cognitive Model**

Cognitive psychologists contend that internal mental processes (such as expectations and awareness of contingencies) play an important role in learned behaviour. Thus according to the cognitive model, abnormal behaviour is best understood as the result of such internal mental processes. Unlike the psycho-analytic model, the cognitive model stresses mental processes of which the individual is aware and sees the individual as an active processor of information. For example, a bright student who considers himself academically inferior to his classmates and who believes that: he doesn't have the ability to perform well on a test may not study for the test with much care or confidence. Naturally, he performs poorly, and his poor performance confirms his belief that he is academically inferior. The student is caught up in a vicious circle in which self-defeating, belief s lead to failure which then further strengthens the self defeating beliefs. To get out of this type of vicious cycle, cognitive psychologists advise that a therapist who sets out to modify abnormal behaviour must first modify the person's cognitive process.

## 4. The Biological Model

The biological model contends that abnormal behaviour is caused at least in part by hereditary factors as well as the malfunctioning of the nervous system and the endocrine glands. Evidence is increasing to the effect that genetic factors are involved in disorders as diverse as schizophrenia, mental retardation, and croninality. Many cases of depression and schizophrenia also seem to stem from disturbances in the biochemistry of the nervous system.

## SECTION (E)
## TYPES OF ABNORMAL BEHAVIOUR

Uptill the end of the last section we have been talking about abnormal behaviour as if it were all of a kind, but there are in fact many different kinds of psychological disorders. Classifying abnormal behaviour into major categories and specific types is not an easy task at all. For about forty-two years, the American Psychiatric Association (APA) has issued an official manual describing and classifying the various types of abnormal behaviour. This publication titled "the Diagnostic and Statistical Manual of Mental Disorders (DSM)", has gone through four editions. The first appeared in 1952, the second in 1968, the third in 1980, and the fourth in 1993. Each edition differs from its predecessors in being more detailed and comprehensive.

But unfortunately, as at the time of writing this text we were not able to have access to the fourth edition of the DSM (DSM – IV – R). As a result, we shall rely on the third edition (DSM – 111 – R) in our subsequent discussion of types of abnormal behaviour in this chapter and in this textbook in general. The major categories of abnormal behaviours and their various specific manifestations are as follows:-

## I.     Anxiety Disorders

**Anxiety disorders** include all the cases of fear and anxiety in which the people do not say why they are afraid or anxious or in which the anxiety is inappropriate to the circumstances. In either case, the person's fear and anxiety don't seem to "make sense".

The clearest examples of anxiety disorders are **panic attacks,** which are sudden, ...................... unpredictable attacks of intense fear or terror. During panic attack, a person may also have feelings of impending doom, chest pain, dizziness or fainting, and a fear of losing control or dying. A panic attack usually lasts only a few minutes, but such attacks recur for no apparent reason. For example:

> *A 31-year-old stewardess had suddenly begun to feel panicky, dizzy, had trouble breathing, started to sweat, and trembled uncontrollably. She excused herself and sat in the back of the plane and within ten minutes the symptoms had subsided. Two similar episodes had occurred to her in the past: the first, four years previously, when the plane had encountered mild turbulence; the second, two years earlier, during an otherwise uneventful flight, as in the present episode (Spitzer et al, 1981, p. 219).*

In contrast to panic attacks, which seem to occur without any obvious cause or triggering event, **posttraumatic stress disorder**, and the name implies, is clearly related to some original stressful event. Examples include people who have lived through fires, flood, tornadoes, close encounters with dangerous animals like snake, armed robbers, or the horrors of military combat may experience episodes of fear and terror some months or year afterwards; sometimes these involve "reliving" the traumatic event.

Another form of anxiety disorder is **obsessive – compulsive disorder**. Obsessions are involuntary thoughts or ideas that keep recurring despite the person's attempt to stop them, **compulsions** are repetitive, ritualistic behaviours that a person feels compelled to perform. For example, a man who checks his watch every five minutes when his wife is late coming home is merely being normally anxious. But a man who feels that he must go through his house every hour checking every clock for accuracy, even though he knows that there is no reason to do so, is showing signs of an obsessive-compulsive disorder.

Finally, **phobic disorders** are also closely linked to feelings of anxiety. A **phobia** is an intense, paralysing fear of something in the absence of any real danger – a fear of something that most other people find bearable. This fear is often recognized by the person suffering from it as unreasonable, but it persists nonetheless.

Of course, many people have irrational fears. Fears of height, water, closed rooms, and cats are all common phobias. But when people are so afraid of snakes that they cannot go to a zoo, walk though a field, or even look at pictures of snakes without trembling, they may be said to have a phobic disorder. Such phobias are generally categorised as **simple** phobias and also include such fears as those of darkness, infections, and even running water.

Perhaps the most common phobic disorder is agoraphobia, "a marked fear of being alone, or being in public places from which escape might be difficult." Sufferers avoid such things as elevators, tunnels, and crowds, especially crowded stores or busy streets. For reasons that are not yet fully understood, most agoraphobics arc women. One possible explanation is the fact that traditionally it has been more acceptable for a woman to be housebound. It is also possible that women more readily admit to the problem.

Another important category of phobias is social phobias, which are fears generally connected with the presence of other people. Fear of public speaking is a social phobia.

For some people, even eating in public can cause severe anxiety. Like agoraphobia, social phobias generally begin during adolescence, when an individual is experiencing growing awareness of his or her interactions with other people.

## TYPES OF PHOBIAS

| S/N | Type | Definition |
|-----|------|------------|
| 1. | Claustrophobia | The fear of being in an enclosure, e.g small room, elevator, etc. |
| 2. | Gynophobia | To be afraid of woman. |
| 3. | Disease phobia | It's the fear of having a disease even with the absence of any symptoms. |
| 4. | Peer group phobia | The state at which an individual finds himself unable to stand boldly among his peer group. |
| 5. | Rupophobia | This involves the fear of dirt. |
| 6. | Lalophobia | The fear of speaking |
| 7. | Ergophobia | The fear of work |
| 8. | Necrophobia | The fear of dead people |
| 9. | Athirophobia | The fear of domestic cats |
| 10. | Homilophobia | The person that fears sermons |
| 11. | Parthenophobia | This means somebody that dreads virgins |
| 12. | Gephryophobia | Somebody that fear crossing water |
| 13. | Melissophobia | Somebody that fears bees |
| 14. | Algophobia | This is a fear of pain or things that causes pain e.g. fight, cat, etc |
| 15. | Bactorio phobia | This is the fear for bacterias |
| 16. | Cynophobia | The people involved in this kind are afraid of dogs. |
| 17. | Ophidiophobia | This is the fear of snakes (reptiles) |
| 18. | Vehicle phobia | This is the fear of entering car, plane, train etc. |
| 19. | Weapon phobia | The fear of harmful weapons like guns, knives, scissors, etc. |
| 20. | Social phobia | The fear which is generally connected with the presence of |

| | | other people. |
|---|---|---|
| 21. | Electro phobia | This is the fear of electricity or the fear of the sparkling of electricity. |
| 22. | Demono phobia | This is the fear of demons and devilish things or spirits. |
| 23. | Simple phobia | This involves the fear of common objects or animals. |
| 24. | Hetero phobia | Fear of having sexual conduct with another person of the opposite sex. |
| 25. | Micro phobia | The fear of small objects. |
| 26. | Counter phobia | It occurs when a person is driven to overcome some particular dangerous challenge. |
| 27. | Nycto phobia | An irritational fear of the dark e.g. being afraid of the night. |
| 28. | Xeno phobia | This involves the fear of foreigners. |
| 29. | Kakorraphia phobia | This states the fear of failure. |
| 30. | Necrophobia | The fear of dead bodies. |
| 31. | Penphobia | The fear of writing for long. |
| 32. | Androphobia | The fear of the presence of man |
| 33. | Taphephobia | The fear of being buried alive. |
| 34. | Hemophobia | The fear of the sight of blood |
| 35. | Muxophobia | For one to be afraid of mices. |
| 36. | Black phobia | The fear of black people |
| 37. | Brontophobia | This is when an individual is afraid of storms. |
| 38. | Insert phobia | This is when an individual is scared of insects like cockroach, mosquitoes, termites, etc. |
| 39. | Acrophobia | This is when an individual is afraid |

| | | |
|---|---|---|
| | | of heights e.g. sky scraper, storey building etc. |
| 40. | Bibliphobia | This is the fear of reading books especially large books. |
| 41. | Anghophobia | A morbid fear or dislike for English people |
| 42. | Agara phobia | This is the fear of being in an open place or in public places. |
| 43. | Phobophobia | This is the fear of fears, the fear being alarmed. |
| 44. | Pantophobia | This is the fear of every thing. |
| 45. | Aerophobia | This is the fear of flying e.g. in aeroplanes etc. |
| 46. | Photo phobia | This is an intense fear of light, that is one cannot look directly at light. |
| 47. | Domaphobia | Fear of being alone in the house |
| 48. | Hydrophobia | This is the fear of water i.e river, streams, sea, etc. |
| 49. | Pynaphobia | The fear of fire. |
| 50. | Sitophobia | This is the dislike of food. |
| 51. | Strasophobia | The fear of standing up |
| 52. | Speed phobia | The fear of being in a high speed while travelling, driving a car etc |
| 53. | Trouble phobia | The fear of facing trouble or stress especially with ones enemy. |
| 54. | Botaphobia | The fear for plants. |
| 55. | Zoo phobia | This is the fear of being among animals. |
| 56. | Sex phobia | The fear which concerns adult to make love with an opposite sex. |
| 57. | Phono phobia | This is the fear of noise e.g. shouts and screams. |

| 58. | Demo phobia | The fear of crowds. |
| 59. | Hemophobia | This involves the fear of the sight of blood. |
| 60. | Alyophobia | The fear of rain |
| 61. | Mogut Are Jpnoa | The fear of bad (horror) dreams at night. |
| 62. | Astraphobia | The fear of thunder or lighting |
| 63. | School phobia | The fear to go to school, the refusal to go to school. |
| 64. | Bathnophobia | The fear of depth. |
| 65. | Thanatophobia | The fear of death |
| 66. | Kaino phobia | The fear of new things |
| 67. | Auto phobia | The fear of solitude |
| 68. | Scopophobia | The fear of being seen |
| 69. | Anmephobia | The fear of winds and drought |
| 70. | Tocophobia | The fear of child birth |

## II.   Somatoform Disorders

Somatoform disorders involve physical symptoms of serious bodily disorders without any physical evidence of organic causes for them. Sufferers from these disorders do not consciously seek to mislead people about their physical condition. The symptoms are real and not under voluntary control.

In cases of **somatization disorder**, the person feels vague, recurring, physical symptoms for which medical attention has been repeatedly sought but no organic cause found. Complaints often involve back pains, dizziness, partial paralysis, abdominal pains, and sometimes anxiety and depression. The following case is typical:  An elderly woman complained of headaches and periods or weakness that lasted for over six months.  Her condition had been evaluated by doctors numerous times: she was taking several prescription medications, and she had actually undergone thirty operations for a variety of complaints. She was thin, but examination showed her to be within normal limits in terms of physical health except for numerous surgical scars). Her medical history spanned half a century, and there can be little doubt that she suffered from somatization disorder (Quill, 1985).

Less often people complain of more bizarre symptoms such as paralysis, blindness, deafness, seizures, less of feeling, or false pregnancy. Sufferers from suck **conversion disorders** have intact muscles and nerves, yet their symptoms are very real. For example, a person with such a "paralyzed" limb has no feeling in it, even if stuck with a pain. A related somatoform disorder is **hypocrondrisis** commonly known as "hypochondria"). In this case, the person interprets some small sign or symptom - perhaps a cough, bruise, or perspiration - as a sign of a serious disease. Although the Symptom may exist," there is no evidence that it reflects a serious illness. Nevertheless, repeated assurance of this sort have little effect, and the person is likely to visit one doctor after another looking for one who will share his or her conviction.

## III.    Psychophysiological Disorders

Psychophysiological disorders are real physical disorders that seem to have psychological causes. Many cases of ulcer, migraine headaches, asthma, high blood pressure, and other disorders are thought to be psychological in origin. In each case, the complaints have a valid physical basis but they are thought-to stem originally from stress, anxiety, and other psychological causes. Indeed, modern medicine is beginning to accept the idea that many physical ailments are to some extent psychophysiological, since stress, anxiety and various states of emotional arousal after body chemistry and the functioning of bodily organs.

It is important to distinguish between psychophysiological disorder is really sick: a hypochondriac is not. In hypochondriasis, the person believes that he or she is seriously ill despite the absence of any substantial symptoms and despite reassurances to the - contrary from physicians. The hypochondriac might almost be said to be suffering from "disease phobia" - fear that he or she has a serious disease.

As we said, however, an individual suffering from a psychophysiological disorder is physically ill. In fact, since virtually every physical disease may be linked to psychologic stress, DSM-III-R does not list all the serious diseases as such. Rather, the manual categorizes psychophysiological disorders according to the part of the body that is affected. For example, psychophysiological respiratory disorders include bronchial asthma and the hiccups; psycho-physiological musculo-skeletal disorders include backache and tension headache.

How can psychological stress lead to physical illness? When people experience stress, their hearts, lungs, and nervous systems, among other bodily functions, are forced to work harder, and it is not surprising that when such conditions are prolonged, a person is more likely to experience some kind of physical debility. For example, stress is known to be an important factor in the development of coronary heart disease (CHD), which is the leading cause of death and disability in this country. Although heredity is also an important factor, even among genetically identified twins the incidence of CHD is linked closely to attitude toward work, problems in the home, and amount of leisure time (Kringlen, 1981). Another study found that Japanese-Americans were more likely to experience CHD than Japanese-Living in Japan; and Japanese-Americans who had embraced American cultural values had a higher rate of CDH than those who followed traditional Japanese cultural values (Marmot & Syme, 1976). We also know that occupation and accompanying stress are also factors in CHD. For instance, London bus drivers are far more likely to have CHD than are the conductors who sell the bus tickets but do not have contend with the strain of driving in heavy traffic. (For and Adelstein, 1978). And among these who have suffered heart attacks for whatever reason, life stress and social isolation have been shown to be significant predictors of survival or mortality (Ruberman et al, 1984).

Thus a great deal of evidence supports the theory of an important relationship between psychological stress and physical illness. Furthermore, the relationship between psychological factors and physical healthsis a two-way street. When you get sick, you are more likely to experience feelings of anxiety or helplessness. Obviously, someone with a serious illness will experience feelings of depression and frustration, but even catching a cold is likely to affect a person psychologically.

## IV.    Dissociative Disorders

Dissociative disorders are among the most puzzling forms of mental disorders, both to the observer and to the sufferer. Dissociation means that part of an individual's personality is separated or dissociated from the rest, and for some reason the person cannot reassemble the pieces. It is usually takes the form of memory loss, a complete - but usually temporary - change in identity, or even the presence of several distinct personalities in one person.

Loss of memory without an organic cause may be a reaction to intolerable experiences. People often block out an event or a period of their lives if it has been extremely stressful. During World War II, some hospitalised soldiers could not recall their names, where they lived, when they were born, or how they came to be in battle. But war and its horrors are not the only causes of **amnesia**. The person who betrays a friend to complete a business deal or the unhappily married man who reserves a single ticket to Tahiti may also forget - selectively - what he has done. He may even assume an entirely new identity, although this phenomenon is unusual.

Total amnesia, in which people forget everything, is quite rare, despite its popularity in novels and films. In one unusual case, the police picked up a 42-year-old man after he became involved in a fight with a customer at the diner where he worked. The man reported that he had no memory of his life before he drifted into town a few weeks earlier. Eventually, he was found to match the description of a missing person who had wandered from his home 200 miles away. Just before he disappeared, he had been passed over for promotion at work and had had a violent argument with his teenage son (Spitzer et al, 1981).

Even rarer and more bizarre than amnesia is the disorder known as **multiple personality,** in which a person has several distinct personalities that emerge at different times. This dramatic disorder, which has been the subject of popular fiction and films, is actually extremely rare. In the true multiple personality, the various personalities are distinct people, with their own names, identities, memories, mannerisms, speaking voices, and even 1Qs. Sometimes, the personalities are so separate that they don't know that they inhabit a body with other "people"; sometimes, personalities do know of the existence of others and will even make disparaging remarks about them. Consider the case of Maud and Sara K., two personalities that coexisted in one woman:

> *In general demeanor, Maud was quite different from Sara. She walked with a swinging, bouncing gait that contrasted to Sara's sedate one. While Sara was depressed, Maud was ebullient and happy... Insofar as she could, dressed differently from Sara.... Sara used no make-up.*

*Maud used a lot of rouge and lipstick, and painted her toenails deep red.... Sara was a mature, intelligent individual. Her mental age was 19.2 years, 1Q, 128. A psychometric done on Maud snowed a mental age of 6.6, IQ, 43 (Coleman et al., 1984, pp. 221-222).*

It is typical for multiple personalities to contrast sharply with each other. It is as if the two (and sometimes more) personalities represent different aspects of a single person - one the more socially acceptable, "nice" personality, the other the darker, more uninhibited or "evil" side.

A far less dramatic (and much more common) dissociative disorder is **depersonalization disorder.** Its essential feature is that the person suddenly feels changed or different in a strange way. Some people feel that they have left their bodies, others that their actions are mechanical or dreamlike. A sense of losing control of one's own behaviour is common, and it is not unusual to imagine changes in one's environment. This kind of feeling is especially common during adolescence and young adulthood, when our sense of ourselves and our interactions with others changes rapidly. Only when the sense of depersonalisation becomes a long-term or chronic problem, or when the alienation impairs normal social functioning, can this be classified as a dissociative disorder (APA, 1980). For example, a 20-year-old college student sought professional help after experiencing episodes of feeling "outside" himself for two years. At these times, he felt groggy, dizzy, and preoccupied. Since he had had several episodes while driving, he had stopped driving alone. Although he was able to keep up with his studies, his friends began be notice chat he seemed "spacy" and self-preoccupied (Spitzer et al., 1981).

Psychoanalytic theorists believe that some dissociative disorders, like amnesia, are the result of person's completely blocking out thoughts or impulses that arouse anxiety (or any associated thoughts that might possibly trigger anxiety). Multiple personality, on the other hand, involves a kind of projection in which each personality can say of the others, in effect, "It's not me who's thanking or saying these terrible things. "Depersonalisation works in much the same way, although much less dramatically.

Behaviourists would not agree that dissociative disorders arise from unconscious conflicts, but they would agree that these behaviours can, under some circumstances, be learned and maintained. They point out that amnesiacs who cannot recall personally important information are frequently individuals who are not well-prepared to deal with emotional conflict; for them, blocking out disturbing thoughts and avoiding stress are rewarding forms of behaviour.

## V.     Affective Disorders

As their name suggests, **affective disorders** are characterized by disturbances in affect, or emotional state. Most people have a wide affective range - that is, they are capable of being happy or sad, animated or quiet, cheerful or discouraged, overjoyed or miserable, depending on the circumstances. In people with affective disorders, this range is greatly restricted. These people seem stuck at one and or the other of the emotional spectrum, either consistently happy or consistently sad, with little regard for the circumstances of their lives. In other cases, they alternate between extremes of happiness and sadness.

The most common affective disorder is **depression,** a state in which a person feels overwhelmed with sadness, grief, and guilt. Depressed people are unable to experience pleasure from activities that they once enjoyed and are tired and apathetic - sometimes to the point of being unable to make the simplest everyday decisions. They may feel as if they have failed utterly in life, and they tend to blame themselves for their problems. Seriously depressed people often have disturbed patterns of sleeping and eating (insomnia is common, and the individual may lose interest in food). In very serious cases, depressed people may be plagued by suicidal thoughts or may even attempt suicide.

It is important to distinguish between the clinical disorder known as depression and the "normal" kind of depression that all people experience from time to time. It is entirely normal to become depressed when a loved one has died, when you've come to the end of a romantic relationship, when you have problems on the job or at school - even when the weather's bad or you don't have a date for Saturday night. Most psychologically healthy people get "the blues" occasionally for no apparent reason. But in all these instances, the depression either is related to a "real world" problem or passes quickly. Only when depression is serious, lasting, and seemingly unrelated to any stressful life event can it be classified as an affective disorder (APA, 1980). For example:

*A 50-year-old widow was transferred to a medical center from her community mental health center, to which she had been admitted three weeks previously with severe agitation, pacing, and hand wringing, depressed mood accompanied by severe self-reproach, insomnia, and a 6-8 kg (15 pound) weight loss. She believed that her neighbours were against her, had poisoned her coffee, and had bewitched her to punish her because of her wickedness. Seven years previously, after the death of her husband, she had required hospitalisation for a similar depression, with extreme guilt, agitation, insomnia, accusatory hallucinations of voices calling her a worthless person, and preoccupation with thoughts of suicide (Spitzer et al., 1981, pp. 28-29).*

But affective disorders do not always involve depression. Less commonly, people experience a state of mania, in which they become hyperactive and excessively talkative, are easily distracted, are euphoric or "high," and seem extremely flamboyant. People in a manic state have unlimited hopes and schemes but often have little interest in carrying them out. They sometimes become aggressive and hostile toward others as their self-confidence becomes more and more unrealistic. In an extreme case, people going though manic episodes may become wild, incomprehensible, or violent until they collapse from exhaustion.

Manic episodes rarely appear by themselves; rather, they usually alternate with depression. Such an affective disorder, in which both mania and depression are present, is known as bipolar disorder (the person alternates between two "poles" or mania and depression). Occasionally, bipolar disorder is seen in a mild form: The person has alternating moods of unrealistically high spirits followed by moderate depression.

## VI.    Personality Disorders

**Personality disorders:** Disorders in which inflexible and maladaptive ways of thinking and behaving cause distress and conflicts. Schizoid personality disorder.

A person's personality is his or her unique and enduring pattern of thoughts, feelings, and behaviour. And we also saw that people normally have the ability to adjust their behaviour to fit the needs of different situations, despite certain characteristic views of the world and ways of doing things. But some people develop inflexible and maladaptive ways of thinking and behaving that are so exaggerated and rigid that they cause serious distress and social problems. People with such **personality disorders** may range from the harmless eccentric to the cold-blooded killer. Recently, it has been estimated that at least half of those who seek help for a psychological problem show some evidence of a personality disorder.

One group of personality disorders is characterized by odd or eccentric behaviour. For example, people who exhibit schizoid personality disorder lack the ability or desire to form social relationships and have no warm or tender feelings for others. Such "loners" cannot express their feelings and are perceived by others as cold, distant, and unfeeling. Moreover, they often appear vague, absentminded, indecisive, or "in a fog". Because their withdrawal is so complete, schizoids seldom marry and may have trouble holding jobs that require them to work with or relate to others (APA, 1980). For example:

> *A 36-year-old electrical engineer was "dragged" to a marital therapist by his wife because of his unwillingness to join in family activities, failure to take an interest in his children, lack of affection, and disinterest in sex... The patient's history revealed long-standing social indifference, with only an occasional and brief friendship here and there (Spitzer et al., 1981, p. 66).*

People with **paranoid** personality disorder also appear to be odd. They are suspicious and mistrustful even when there is no reason to be, and are hypersensitive to any possible threat or trick. They refuse to accept blame or criticism even when it is deserved. They are guarded, secretive, devious, scheming, and argumentative, although they often see themselves as rational and objective. In one case, for example, a construction worker began to get into disputes with his co-workers because he was afraid that they might let his scaffolding slip in order to kill or injure him. Upon examination by a psychologist, he thought that his examiner was "taking their side" against him (Spitzer et al., 1981, p. 37).

A second cluster of personality disorders is characterized by dramatic, emotional, or erratic behaviour. For example, people with narcissistic personality disorder display nearly total self-absorption, a grandiose sense of self-importance, a preoccupation with fantasies of unlimited success, a need for constant attention and admiration, and an inability to love or really care for anyone else. The world **narcissism** comes from a character in Greek mythology named narcissus, who fell in love with his own reflection in a pool and pined away because he could not reach the beautiful face that he saw before him. For example, a male graduate student sought help because he was having difficulty completing his Ph.D dissertation. He bragged that his dissertation would revolutionise his field and make him famous – but he had not been able to write much of it yet. He blamed his academic adviser for his lack of progress, called his fellow students "drones," and stated that everyone was jealous of his brilliance. He had frequent brief relationships with women, but few lasting friendships. Although excess self-esteem would seem to be the prominent problem here, this may not be the case. Otto Kernberg observes that the self-esteem of the narcissistic person is really very fragile. The pathological narcissist cannot sustain his or her self-regard without having it fed constantly by the attentions of others.

Many psychologists believe that narcissism begins early in life. While all infants tend to be narcissistic, most grow out of it. But for reasons that we do not yet understand, the narcissistic person never makes the change. Some social critics assert that certain tendencies in modern society – such as our worship of youth and beauty and our disregard for old age – have contributed to an apparent "boom" In narcissistic personality disorders (Lasch, 1979). Clinical data, however, do not support this speculation, While acknowledging that our society stimulates narcissism, Kernberg argues that this cannot be the root of the disorder: "The most I would be willing to say Is that society can make serious psychological abnormalities, which already exist in some percentage of the population, seem to be at least superficially appropriate" (Wolfe, 1978, p. 59).

One of the most widely studied personality disorders is antisocial personality disorder. People who exhibit this disorder lie, steal, cheat, and show little or no sense of responsibility, although often they are intelligent and charming on first acquaintance. The "con man" exemplifies many of the features of the antisocial personality, as does the man who compulsively cheats his business partners because he knows their weak points. The antisocial personality rarely shows the slightest trace of anxiety or guilt over his or her behaviour. Indeed, these people blame society or their victims for the antisocial actions that they themselves commit.

Unfortunately, antisocial personalities are often responsible for a good deal of crime and violence, as seen in this case history of an antisocial personality:

Although intelligent, the subject was a poor student and was frequently accused of stealing from his schoolmates. At the age of 14, he stole a car, and at the age of 20, he was imprisoned for burglary. After he was released, he spent another two years in prison for drunk driving and then eleven years for a series of armed robberies.

Released from prison yet one more time in 1976, he tried to hold down several jobs but succeeded at none of them. He moved in with a woman whom he had met one day earlier, but he drank heavily (a habit that he had picked up at age 10) and struck her children until she ordered him out of the house at gunpoint. On at least two occasions, he violated his parole but was not turned in by his parole officer. In July of 1976, he robbed a service station and shot the attendant twice in the head. He was apprehended in part because he accidentally shot himself during his escape. "It seems like things have always gone had for me," he later said. "It seems like I've always done dumb things that just caused trouble for me" (Spitzer et al., 1983, 1983, p. 68).

Under psychiatric evaluation, he was found to have a superior 1Q of 129 and a remarkably good store of general knowledge. He slept and ate well and exhibited no significant changes of mood. He admitted to having "made a mess of my life" but added that "I never stew about the things I have done".

The subject was named Gary Gilmore, and on January 17, 1977, he was the first person to be executed in the United States in eleven years. While awaiting an execution that was postponed several times, he became the subject of numerous news stories detailing his fight for his announced "right to be executed." He twice attempted suicide.

Perhaps 3 percent of American men and less than I percent of American women suffer from antisocial personality disorder. However, it is very difficult to make sound judgements about the prevalence of this disorder because the only reliable laboratory setting so far has been the prison. One study categorized 50 percent of the populations of two prisons as antisocial personalities (Hare, 1983), but other studies show that many of the most common criteria also apply to large numbers of people raised in economically deprived environments. One researcher placed the following advertisement. In an underground Boston newspaper:

> WANTED: *charming, aggressive, carefree people who are impulsively irresponsible but are good at handling people and at looking after Number One. Send name,*

*address, phone, and short biography proving how interesting you are... (Widom, 1978, p. 72).*

Of 73 respondents, about one-third seemed to satisfy the typical criteria for antisocial personality disorder. Widom was forced to conclude that about the only difference between prison samples and the people in her own study was the fact that her subjects had somehow' avoided being apprehended-by the police.

Not surprisingly, these same problems complicate efforts to explain antisocial behaviour. Some psychologists feel that it is the result of emotional deprivation in early childhood. Respect for others is the basis of our social code, but if you cannot see things from the other person's perspective, rules about what you can and cannot do will seem to be only an assertion of adult power to be broken as soon as possible. The child for whom no one cares, say psychologists, cares for no one. The child whose problems no one identifies with can identify with no one else's problems.

Social learning theorists base, their explanations on the nature of family influences. They reason that a person who has been rejected bygone or both parents is not likely to develop adequate social skills and appropriate social behaviour. They also point out the high incidence of antisocial behaviour in people with an antisocial parent and suggest that antisocial behaviour may in part be a result of modelling that parent's behaviour (Robins, 1966).

Cognitive theorists emphasize the role of arrested moral development. For example, between the ages of about 7 and II, all children are apt to respond to unjust treatment by behaving unjustly toward someone else who is vulnerable. At about age 13, however, they are better able to reason in abstract terms, and most children begin to think more in terms of fairness than vindictiveness. This seems to be especially true if new cognitive skills and moral concepts are reinforced by parents and peers (Berkowitz & Gibbs, 1983). From this standpoint, cognitive psychologists feel that antisocial behaviour is the result of development arrested during the period at which children do not estimate the effects of their behaviour on other people.

An entirely different perspective seeks the roots of antisocial personality disorder in biology. For example, there is some evidence that the impulsive and aggressive tendencies characteristic of antisocial behaviour correlate with abnormalities in the brain (Hill, 1952). Impulsive violence and aggression have also been linked with abnormal levels of certain neurotransmitters (Virkkunen, 1983). Other findings suggest that heredity is a factor in the development of antisocial behaviour (Bonham et al., 1982; Hutchings & Mednick, 1977). Although none of this research is definitive, it does suggest that some antisocial personalities may be victims of their nervous systems as much as of their upbringings - an explanation that we have seen repeatedly throughout this chapter.

## VII.   Schizophrenic Disorders

It is a common misconception that schizophrenia means "split personality." This is not the case at all. The disorder commonly meant by the term split personality is actually multiple personality disorder, which, as we have seen, is a dissociative disorder. The misunderstanding comes from the fact that the root schizo - comes from the Greek verb meaning "to split." But what is split in schizophrenia is not so much the personality as the mind itself.

**Schizophrenic disorders** are marked by disordered thought and communication, inappropriate emotions, and bizarre behaviour that last for months. Schizophrenics are out of touch With reality. They often suffer from hallucinations, (false sensory perceptions) which most often take the form .of hearing voices - although some schizophrenics experience visual, tactile, or olfactory hallucinations. Schizophrenics usually have delusions (false beliefs about reality with no factual basis) that distort their relationships with their surroundings and with other people. They may think that a doctor wishes to kill them or that they are receiving radio messages from outer space. They often regard their own bodies - as well as the outside world - as hostile and alien. Because their world is utterly different from the one most people live in, they usually cannot live anything like a normal life. Often, they are unable to communicate with others, for when they speak, their words are a total confusion.

See Table 14-2 for the DSM-III-R criteria for schizophrenia. The following case illustrates some of schizophrenia's characteristic features.

*(The patient is a 35-year-old widow.) For many years she has heard voices, which insult her and cast suspicion on her chastity... The voices are very distinct, and in her opinion, they must be carried by a telescope or a machine from her home. Her thoughts are dictated to her; she is obliged to think them, and hears them repeated after her. She... has all kinds of uncomfortable sensations in her body, to which something is "done". In particular, her "mother parts" are turned inside out, and people send a pain through her back, lay ice-water on her heart, squeeze her neck, injure her spine, and violate, her. There are also hallucinations of sight - black figures and the altered appearance of people - but these are far less frequent... (Spitzer et al., 1981, pp. 308-309).*

There are actually several kinds of schizophrenic disorders, which differ from one another in terms of characteristic symptoms.

**Disorganized schizophrenia** includes some of the more bizarre symptoms, such as giggling, grimacing, and frantic gesturing. People suffering from disorganized schizophrenia show a childish disregard for social conventions and may urinate or defecate at inappropriate times. They are active but aimless, and they are often given to incoherent conversations.

The primary feature of catatonic schizophrenia is a severe disturbance of motor activity. People in this state may remain immobile, mute, and impassive. At the opposite extreme, they become excessively excited, talking and shouting continuously. They may behave in a robo-like fashion when ordered to move, and some have even let doctors mold their arms and legs into strange and uncomfortable positions that they then can maintain for hours.

**Paranoid schizophrenia** is marked by extreme suspiciousness and quite complex delusions. Paranoid schizophrenics may believe themselves to be Napoleon or the Virgin Mary or may insist that Russian spies with laser guns are constantly on their trail because they have learned some great secret. These people may actually, appear more "normal" than other schizophrenics if their delusions are compatible with everyday life; they are less likely to be incoherent or to look or act "crazy." However, they may become hostile or aggressive toward anyone who questions their thinking or tries to contradict their delusions (Sarason & Sarason, 1987).

Finally, **undifferentiated schizophrenia** refers to those people who have several of the characteristic symptoms of schizophrenia, such as delusions, hallucinations, or incoherence, yet do not show the typical symptoms of any other subtype.

Since schizophrenia is both common mental disorder and a very serious one, considerable research has been directed at trying to discover its causes. As we saw in Chapter 2, it is now clear from a wide range of studies that there is some genetic component to schizophrenia. People who are schizophrenic are more likely than other people to have schizophrenic children, even when those children have lived with foster parents since birth (Heston, 1966). And if an identical twin becomes schizophrenic, the chances are about 50 percent that the other twin will also become schizophrenic; but if a fraternal twin becomes schizophrenic, the chances are only about 10 percent that the other twin will also become schizophrenic (Rosenthal, 1970). But note that even with Identical twins, who are genetically exactly the same, half of the twins of schizophrenics do not themselves become schizophrenic.

These studies and others indicate that some kind of biological predisposition to schizophrenia is inherited (McGuffin, Reveley, Holland, 1982; Zerbin-Rudin, 1972). Recent research suggests that the problem may lie in excess amounts of dopamine in the central nervous system. Drugs that alleviate schizophrenic symptoms also decrease the amount of dopamine in the brain and block dopamine receptors. On the other hand, amphetamines increase the amount of dopamine in the brain, increase the severity of schizophrenic symptoms, and if taken in excess lead to what is called "amphetamine psychosis," which is very similar to schizophrenia.

However, research indicates that many people who are genetically vulnerable to schizophrenia do not become schizophrenic. Environmental factors - in particular, disturbed family relations - are also involved in determining whether a person will become schizophrenic. McGuffin, Reveley, and Holland (1982) reported on a set of identical triplets who all suffered from chronic psychotic disorders. But while two brothers had clear and severe schizophrenic symptoms and were unable to function between psychotic periods, the third brother was able to function at a higher level and hold down a job between periods. His 1Q was higher and his relationship with his family less trouble. Environment and experience can increase or decrease the effects of any inherited tendency, and the result is often a significant difference between two individuals' levels of functioning.

Along these same lines, a number of studies have demonstrated a relationship between social class and schizophrenia (Hollingshead & Redlich, 1958). In general, the incidence of schizophrenia is decidedly higher in the lower class than in other social classes. One theory holds that the lower-class socio-economic environment, offering little education, opportunity, or reward, is a cause of schizophrenia; another holds that the motivational and cognitive impairments suffered by schizophrenics subject them to a downward social "drift" into lower classes. There appears to be some truth to both theories, but no causal link has been firmly established.

Similarly, some psychologists regard family relationship as a factor in the development of schizophrenia. The evidence in support of this position is mixed. It is true that schizophrenics experience more parental conflicts than other people, and communication between their parents is inferior to that of parents of non-schizophrenics (Fontana, 1966). And one study found that communication problems between parents themselves was an effective predictor of schizophrenia in their children (Goldstein & Rodnick, 1975). And it is clear that families have a significant impact on patients' adjustment after they leave the hospital (Left, 1976). It is much less clear exactly how all of these family factors combine with biological predispositions so that some people but not others experience schizophrenia. That is the continuing challenge of research not only into schizophrenic disorders but into all other forms of abnormal behaviour.

Although quite different in emphasis, the various views of schizophrenic disorders are by no means mutually exclusive. Many theorists believe that a combination of some or all of these factors produces schizophrenia, and in practice, many psychologists use a combination of drugs and therapy to treat schizophrenia. Most psychologists consider the diathesis-stress model to be the most useful theory for further research into the causes of schizophrenia. Genetic factors predispose some people to schizophrenia, and stress activates the predisposition. Unfortunately, the exact sources of stress have not yet been pinned down.

# BIBLIOGRAPHY

Beals, R.L.; Hoijer, H. and Beals, A.R. **An Introduction to Anthropology**. Sixth Edition. Collier Macmillan Publishers: London, England.

Bottomore, T.B. (1962). **Sociology: A Guide to Problems and Literature**. George Allen and Unwin Ltd: London, England.

Broom, L. and Selznick, P. (1977). **Sociology: A Text With Adapted Readings**. Fifth Edition. Harper and Row Publishers, Inc: New York, U.S.A.

Cyril I.D. Clark (1985). **Collective Behaviour and Social Movements**. Koda, Benin City, Nigeria.

Cyril I.D. Clark (1985). **Handbook of Concepts Used in Psychology and Other Behavioural Sciences**. Omega, Benin City, Nigeria.

Hilgard, Ernest R.; Atkinson, Rita L. and Atkinson, Richard C. (1979). **Introduction to Psychology**. Seventh Edition. Harcourt Brace Jovanovich, Inc.: New York, U.S.A.

Hollander, E.P. (1976). **Principles and Methods of Social Psychology**. Oxford University Press: New York, U.S.A.

Krech, D.; Crutchfield, R.S. and Ballanchey, E.L. (1962). **Individual in Society: A Textbook of Social Psychology**. McGraw-Hall Book Company, Inc.: New York, U.S.A.

Kuppuswamy, B. (1979). **Elements of Social Psychology.** Vikas: New Delhi, India.

Kurt W. Back *et al* (1977). **Social Psychology.** John Wiley and Sons: New York, U.S.A.

Liebert, Robert M. and Neale, John M. (1977). **Psychology.** John Wiley and Sons, Inc.: New York, U.S.A.

Lindzey, George and Aronson Elliot (Editors), (1954, 1968). **The Handbook of Social Psychology**. Addison – Wesley Publishing Company: Reading, Mass, U.S.A.

McKee, James B. (1974). **Introduction to Sociology**. 2nd Edition. Holt, Rine Hart and Winston, Inc.: New York, U.S.A.

Mednick, Sarnoff A.; Higgins, Jerry and Kirschebaum, Jack (1975). **Psychology: Explorations in Behaviour and Experience.** John Wiley and Sons, Inc.: New York, U.S.A.

Morris, Charles G. (1988). **Psychology: An Introduction**. Sixth Edition. Prentice Hall, Englewood Cliffs, New Jersey 07632, U.S.A.
Newcomb, T.M.; Turner, R.H. and Converse, P.E. (1965). **Social Psychology: The Study of Human Interaction.** Holt, Rinehart, and Winston Inc.: New York, U.S.A.

Raven, B.H. and Rubin, J.Z. (1975). **Social Psychology: People in Groups**. John Wiley and Sons Inc.: New York, U.S.A.

Secord, P.F.; Backman, C.W. and Slavitt, D.R. (1976). **Understanding Social Life: An Introduction to Social Psychology**. McGraw-Hill Book Company: New York, U.S.A.

Seveoy, L.J.; Brigham, J.C. and Schlenker, B.R. (1976). **A Contemporary Introduction to Social Psychology**. McGraw-Hill Book Company: New York, U.S.A.

Sperling, Abraham P. (1982). **Psychology Made Simple**. Heineman: London, England.

Wrightsman, Lawrence S. (1977). **Social Psychology.** Second dition. Books/Cole Publishing Company: Monterey, Calif., S.A.

oung, Knimball (1957). **Handbook of Social Psychology.** Rev. Edition. Routledge and Kegan Paul, Ltd.: London, England.

www.ingramcontent.com/pod-product-compliance
Lightning Source LLC
Chambersburg PA
CBHW072116270326
41931CB00010B/1572

* 9 7 8 1 8 4 5 4 9 4 9 6 4 *